C0-ASA-653

"MY ADVENTURES WITH MANKIND"

A Layman's Profile of the Bible

by
James P. Whitlock

ST. JOHNS EPISCOPAL CHURCH
211 N. MONROE STREET
TALLAHASSEE, FL 32303

Desert Ministries, Inc.
Fort Lauderdale, Florida

B1
W

4380

MY ADVENTURES WITH MANKIND
A Layman's Profile of the Bible

First Printing
Copyright © 1991
Desert Ministries, Inc.
P.O. Box 2001
Fort Lauderdale, Florida 33303

ISBN 0-914733-15-X

Printed by:
Riverside Press, Inc.
1219 N.E. 4th Avenue
Fort Lauderdale, Florida 33304

Flying Since 1821

"MAY THE FOUR WINDS BLOW YOU SAFELY HOME"

O'Leary, Brooklyn, N.Y.

1989

Table of Contents

James Palmer Whitlock

(In Memoriam)

Sadly, the author of this wonderful book died while it was in its final stages of preparation. It was Jim's wish, supported now by his family and friends and the Board of Desert Ministries, Inc., that the publication be accomplished. Here it is!

Born in Elizabeth, New Jersey, Mr. Whitlock graduated from Princeton University in 1938. He served as Lieutenant Commander in Naval Intelligence during World War II.

He entered the family business, Whitlock Cordage Company, in New York City, and served in sales for many years. Mr. Whitlock also worked for Jones and Laughlin Steel Company and wrote extensively in his time at BBDO Advertising Agency.

Jim was always an active Church Man, serving as Trustee of the Westminster Presbyterian Church in Elizabeth. He also was a regular participant in the Bay Head Chapel in Bay Head, New Jersey, where much of the writing of this book was done. The Whitlocks spent summers together in Mantoloking, New Jersey, on the engaging East Avenue.

Jim and Barbara have three sons and one daughter: James P. Jr., David F., Chester A., and Nancy A., and five grandchildren.

We are especially grateful to Barbara Whitlock, to Donald Stires and the Board of the Bay Head Chapel, and to DMI Board Member John R. Holland for significant contributions which aided us in the publication of this volume.

A Word from the Editor

Jim Whitlock was and is my friend. He has been gone from our sight for nearly a year, but his words and memory stand still in the forefront of my mind. I miss him.

Jim had the gift of appreciation. The smallest mention that he was on the right track or that this book would be helpful to lay readers everywhere cheered him on and prompted a generous note of thanks. My files of Whitlock correspondence and various editions of what follows are voluminous. I saved every word.

Jim was intelligent, well-educated, sensitive and kind. While he was humble, he had the tenacity to stand his ground especially in the writing of this book. I often said, in the peace and calm of his East Avenue porch, that he should consider this change or an alteration of that idea. He appeased me but re-wrote so cleverly that before I knew it, he was back where he had started.

He had a dream, born of his belief that most lay people, and some professionals, do not know the Bible. Worse, they too often do not care. The following pages are his attempt to share a personal search to uncover the genius and grace of the Scriptures and to share them with the expected readers. It is intended for lay people of all varieties of the faith. Theologians and preachers would do well to listen in for his insights are deep and refreshing.

Jim knew how to write, as you will see. He caught the essential power of the people in the Bible and became a channel in "translating" their words and the word of God into a memorable experience. He found the essential unity of the sixty-six books of the Holy Scriptures. He once referred to the Bible as the story of God's Wild Journey with Mankind. It is the presentation of a God who loves His people so much he cannot let them go.

We are proud to offer this remarkable book to the reading public.

Richard M. Cromie, D.D.
President, Desert Ministries, Inc.

Author's Introduction

I have listened to a large number of preachers for more than sixty years, some popular and prestigious, some in huge churches, some in tiny chapels. I mean no disrespect to any of them whatsoever. But, after all those long decades, and some long long sermons, I came to a point in my life, advancing in years, when I still did not know what the Bible was trying to say. What did it mean, to me and mine?

I suppose if you had asked me then, when I began this search ten years ago or so, I would have guessed that I had missed what these vaunted preachers had said or meant to say. After all, the primary purpose of the preaching pastor is to declare the Word of God. Occasionally I was entranced by their words and pulpit magic, but honestly, other than feeling guilty for what I had failed to do, or worse for what I had actually done, I never learned much from all these men whom I admired, and admire still. I served the Church, attended it, and supported it. I was called a leader in it, but still I did not know the Bible.

I wondered secretly, when I thought about it, what those pastors were about. Was the weekly sermon, "a term paper every seven days," as one of them called it, an exercise in filling up the time, or gyrating to the Christian seasons which I have never, and still do not understand? I would give more than a wooden nickle to anyone who can tell me what an Epiphany is, or was, and why there are so many "Sundays after Easter." And still, "Pentecost" amazes me.

One day, I was shocked into silence when I turned for help to my family Bible, which I revered for sure, but I did not know how to get to where it could help me. So I set out to rectify my inadequacies, pronto! This present study, personal, arduous, unfinished, began on the day I learned that a member of our family had a potentially dangerous health problem. The advent of that pressing force forced me to look at everything I was and believed. I promised God then, the Creator and Preserver of us all, that I would spend whatever time it took to learn, and to pass along to others, the enigma which we call the Scriptures, or the Word of God...if we could strike a friendly deal. We did. I kept my promise; and, you should not be surprised, God has kept His.

What follows is the beginning volume of my search to understand the Word I had been told was Holy Writ. You might find it helpful. I hope so. You might find it reads as more gibberish. I remind you I am not a preacher, nor a professional theologian. I am a layman, given some gifts to seek out answers, or perhaps better, to ask questions. I have done both for nearly a decade, maybe more, of course following on years and years of reverent inattentiveness.

The research and writing of this book, which I fear now will never reach its completion before my days are through, began on an important day of my life, but oddly, it has made all my days important ever since. What began as a familial promise to the Lord, "I would keep working if He would keep blessing us," has led me to libraries, endless conversations and communication with preachers and theologians untold, and with lay folks of any and all denominations. These have been helpful to me including some dear and kindly neighbors, and the preachers who have visited our parlor.

I thank my wife, Barbara, our children and grandchildren, who in various measure were and are the reason for this quest. I thank all the pastors who have intoned their illustrious words at, and beyond me, for far longer than any of us care to remember. I guess, as any parent knows, eventually the repetition, usually unheard consciously, finally sinks in—and no matter what we do, our children do grow up. I have grown in this juvenile process.

I thank many others, but most especially my friend, Dick Cromie, of Bay Head, New Jersey, and Fort Lauderdale, Florida, who has guided, and I might add, guarded me, in the whole long and tiring process. He is my friend, has been, and ever more shalt be. There are many others to thank, but without Cromie's golden words, kindly inspiration, and an occasional kick in the shins, I might never have finished the project. (Or have we finished, yet?)

I hope and pray you will find it useful. Its writing, and the reading and re-reading many times over, have been a worthwhile help to me and the others who have seen it, who have been kind enough to say so. God bless you, reader friend. I will see you in the morning....

Whitlock
Autumn, 1989

God Reveals Plot of New Book

"MY CHILDREN AND MY SON'S GOOD FRIENDS HELPED TO WRITE IT"

"I got them to write a book about me, He says. I felt I had a blockbuster story. Maybe even the makings of a best seller," God said from His heavenly realm.

"We assigned our best men to develop the script. And ladies too. Moses was one of the senior editors. He put the Torah together. The first five books, Genesis through Deuteronomy. Great job. David wrote many of the Psalms. There were also Isaiah, Jeremiah, Daniel and many other prophets. In fact most of their passages are my own words.

"They gave me a difficult time about the title. I wanted it to be, 'My Adventures With Man.' My credo is 'What God Can Do for Man.'

"At our meeting to resolve the question, in the heavenly courts I did not pull rank...I was out-voted and we settled on 'The Bible,' which has been favorably accepted.

The concluding chapters were written by good friends of my Son, such as Matthew, Mark, John and Peter. Apostle Paul deserves special mention. He wrote the series of letters which elaborate on the biographies. Luke was a careful historian. His books, Luke and The Acts of the Apostles, are essential."

TWO-THIRDS JEWISH

ONE-THIRD CHRISTIAN

Your Christian Bible. Flip the Pages. Next time you go to church, lift a Bible out of its rack, or better pick it up at home, on a quiet evening.

The first two-thirds of it are the Jewish Books. A true copy of the Bible Jews use today. The ancient Hebrew Holy Scriptures. Abraham, Jacob, Joseph; Moses, David, Isaiah, Micah. All the top players. Along with a harvest of references, many oblique, to a coming king, a new ruler, a Prince, an anointed one, a messiah.

Christians Share Those Scriptures.

The final third of the volume is the story of Jesus Christ. Our New Testament. The Christian document. The Jesus Christ perception of spiritual devotion.

How come the Jewish chronicle finds a place in our Christian Bible alongside and running ahead of Jesus' story? Because without the first you would not have the second.

The clues are there. "A new king, a new ruler, an anointed one, a messiah." These are the Holy Scripture, which tell the journey of God's chosen people, and signals forecasting the coming of Jesus Christ, One anointed by God. Messiah is the Hebrew word for "anointed." Christ is the Greek variation of the good Old Testament word. Could it mainly be that God wanted us to be together, to share a common destiny?

Book One

Chapter I – Prologue:
Some Introductory Essays

Greetings, good friend. We introduce
THE BIBLE, A VOLUME

The first book you come to in this set of two is the Old Testament, a direct copy of the ancient and enduring Jewish Holy Scriptures, still on the job today. Eight hundred pages, half a million words, comprising two-thirds of our Christian Bible. Two thousand years' travel time. A tortuous, exhausting trip that touches all bases but misses home plate. It is a gut-buster.

The New Testament will follow later.

BIBLE
A Panorama

There is today a big trouble with the Bible. Many people do not open it. They are scared to. Therefore, they do not know what is in it. Many passages are incoherent to everyday lay people. Accordingly, they are unable to understand it and come out with a clear picture. Widely, for most people, the Bible remains a closed book.

The laity, the everyday reader, will understand this proposition. Additionally, however, there is small doubt that the clergy are unaware of this difficulty. The leaders of the church often know the Volume like the backs of their hands. Yet there remains the communication hazard, as though either the Bible, in particular the Old Testament, or the public were wearing blindfolds. One speaks in an often difficult and obscure language and the other cannot translate.

The present essay distills the core-plot of the Volume in the next few paragraphs. Later essays will enlarge the developments.

The main events of the Old Testament are accounts of the flow and ebb of God's attempts to achieve His goal...that mankind be a reflection of His image. "I will make man in my own image," He says in Genesis 1:27. This statement says, in effect, 'I want man to be representative of me on earth.'

God made four attempts to reach His goal. Man failed in each instance. The first time was Adam and Eve. They failed...to temptation. God therewith chased them out of the Garden of Eden. Secondly, following Adam and Eve, God bred thousands of people. These masses also missed his intended purpose. He drowned them all in a deep, wet flood. Thirdly, starting anew with Noah and his descendants, in particular with Abraham, God generated a whole new population. These, too, failed, swamped in moral turpitude. God disposed of them in bloody land battles in which Assyria, Babylonia and other countries defeated and captured God's chosen subjects, the Jews and the 'family' of Abraham. The Nation of Israel and its citizens were wiped out.

So fourthly, a handful of Jews returned, as in the Flood-Noah-Ark scenario. They in turn bred many more thousands. A big, big population. However, these, too, also failed in spite of the Ten Commandments and the pleas and warnings of God, spoken through the prophets. As these people also flounder and fail, God threw up his hands in dismay.

The Lord then activated a proposition he had considered many centuries earlier, about 2,000 B.C., and had made veiled reference to in Genesis 12:2 and 3, to wit: "Abraham, your 'family' will be a blessing to all mankind. I will bless you. And you in turn, will be a blessing to me."

To do it, God decided to come to earth Himself and rub shoulders with his people in the Presence of Jesus Christ. This the "Blessing" factor. And eventually it succeeds. But it took a once-in-a-lifetime event to get the point across. The climax is represented in the contiguous acts of crucifixion-resurrection-ascension and the reappearances of Jesus after his temporal death. The Christian concept was born.

God spent the entire Old Testament, two thousand years of it, to reach His climax decision, its results recounted in the New Testament. He was very patient—and very determined—to succeed and attain his objective.

God in His infinite wisdom
God in His infinite patience.

The Bible

It looks like a book.
It feels like a book.
It opens like a book.
You buy it like a book.
But, it is *not* a book.

It is a library.
Biblos, in Greek, is The Book.
Here it is plural.

It is a collection of writings.
A selection of sixty-six scripts composed by
fifty authors, more or less, whose active
lives and works span fifteen hundred
years, more or less.
Ancient editors gathered these ancient
manuscripts - some four thousand years
old - and offered them to the public as a
single, integrated unit. After long and bit-
ter arguments, the Canon (the approved
list of Biblical books) came to be.
They named their presentation, or rather it
was named for them, the Holy Books, or
on the front page, the Holy Bible, with
copyright to Thomas Nelson, or others.
It actually belongs to God.

THE HOLY BIBLE

The difficulty with this volume -
It is long.
It is wordy.
It has many detours,

It bewilders the average person.

People tip-toe around it.
It intimidates.

It is complex,
With all its pages and words and ideas and images.

* * * *

It took a dedicated person,
Not without education or experience,
Three years, five years, seven years
Of intense daily study, examination and analysis,
Under expert leadership and guidance to find the way
Professional students, preparing for ordination
Spend more than that
Before they are ordained —
At college; Seminary graduation exercises
To become an accredited
Priest, minister, clergy.

And even then, twenty years later,
These people still say
With a tolerant smile,
"Oh, my goodness."

* * * *

They expect you to solve it
By going to church on Sundays?

Never!

Chapter II
The Story-Line — Old Version

When you open the pages of the Bible, the sight strikes you as a hammer blow. Three-quarters of a million words blanketing fourteen hundred closely lined, tightly paragraphed pages. Flutter the leaves. Your heart sinks, your resolve shrinks. All you see is black and white and words without end.

Now, suppose your purpose is to compose a digest, or a summary of this work, for an everyday layman, which mine is. How do you cope with such a problem? Where do you start? The sheer volume of material overwhelms you. Its mass can terrify you.

You do the only thing possible. You take it apart, as a good mechanic does, study the relationships, then put it back together, using only the main parts at first: The body, the steering column, the motor drive, the brakes, the lights. All the frills come later on.

You assemble your own set of essays. You check with everyone you know, or who will listen. Your new product now becomes a demonstrator. Test drive it. Place your order for a current model.

*   *   *   *

In the following presentation, the Holy Lands of the Bible become God's proving grounds, His testing ground, a launching pad, a Cape Canaveral of antiquity. At issue is the frailty of man's unpredictable human nature, with more than a pinch of sin built in, facing the challenge of the Lord's self-avowed sublime decree to "make man in His image." With these words God said He would teach man to be a reflection of His purposes and principals. Image means a mirror-reflection. Look at yourself. Do you look like God? Probably not! But God thinks you do. That's what matters.

This is a tall order, indeed. As man faces God's exalted order, he becomes a contestant in the "game" of God's lofty challenge; so does the woman, with uneven results for both.

The two parties, God's challenge and man's frailty, appear poised in adversarial stance. This is a reasonable observation. Behind us is God's disappointing opening experience with Adam and Eve, who flaunting His suggestions, commands, and directives, were banished forever to the East of Eden. I read someplace that man has an instinctive disposition to disobey God. Adam and Eve are the image of us all, not God!

The Intent of the Bible

The Old Testament is the story of how God first made friends with man, and how God came to know and help him. The Bible is the story of God. If there had never been a Bible, we would know next to nothing about God, and nothing about Jesus, the Christ. But old timers, ancient Hebrew Jews, wrote it down. We have the documents we need: The Old Testament and the New Testament. This volume of testimony has been acclaimed for hundreds of generations and four thousand years. The *essential* events actually took place, and you can bet your life and your inner peace on that. Why not? Perhaps it is a gamble, as Pascal said, but you cannot lose in either case.

As an aside, you may like to consider an additional thought for speculation: to wit, God took no chance that this book would not be written. For, from His point of view He could well ask, "Where would I be if there was no Bible?" That is the bottom line of inspiration!

Ancient and modern Jews, and others, have some reasonable questions about the Second Act, the Jesus Christ part of the story. But this is of small consequence. God gives each person the right to his own opinion. Incidentally, and importantly, as you will see, it was the powerful, conniving priests, who were the first to bend any law to nourish their own selfish ends, who snared Jesus into the crucifixion syndrome. Yes, disciple Judas was a Jew, but he was nothing more than a sneaky mole for the threatened, anxious and nervous priests and Pharisees of the day. Judas committed suicide when his betrayal struck his heart. The innocent and "ignorant" everyday Jewish citizen had no part in the plot which led to Jesus' trial, torment and bodily torture. That is for sure. One must be careful of saying that Judas was a Jew, for Jesus also was.

The essential elements of Jesus' life actually took place and are documented by the reinforcing accounts of the four individual writers, and those on whom they depended. To the very end, despite evident and published trust in God and Jesus, many people continue to carry lingering secret doubts or questions—"Did it really happen; it is really true?"

When you become reasonably familiar and comfortable with the factual *essential elements* of the two Testaments, you arrive at a conclusion that bears on revelation: *Aha, the story is true!* One simply cannot avoid the evidence. When you know these things and translate the elements and events into an integrated whole, you have heard your final Sunday sermon, and can go out and preach your own.

You won't need to be told time and again "God is love" or "God loves you." When you see that when God said to Abraham, "Follow me. Trust me. I will lead you," a compact was formed between man and God.

Secondly, when you acknowledged that Abraham's family actually became the Nation of Israel, the compact became a contract. God led. Abraham trusted. Both signed. A deal was closed.

God also declared during the Genesis message to Abraham, "You—your people—will become *a blessing to all mankind.*" God inserted the word *bless* three times during His declaration. Did He have a purpose? With His soft and subtle use of "bless" God may well have been implying the possibility of a coming saviour, as yet unnamed. With the eventual emergence of Jesus Christ among Abraham's people, God's voluntary initiative, made 2,000 years before the fact, came full circle to reality.

Apostle Saint Paul acknowledged this circumstance in his letter to the Galatian people, circa 50 A.D.

Understand that God announced the Gospel in advance to Abraham with the words: "All mankind will be blessed through you." GALATIANS 3:8

When you grasp the magnificence of these matters, you hold in the palm of your hand the essence, the nucleus, the very embryo of the Bible story, and the secret meaning of your days and decades on the earth. Nothing whatever can take this insight away. Like Paul's love in I Corinthians 13, it never ends.

An Aside...
"It Was No Accident, My Friend."

The three of them had been batting ides back and forth about incidents in the Bible.

"You mean God planned it that way?" exclaimed Mary.

"Absolutely," answered John. "It was deliberate. It was the only way He could make sure things would come out right."

"I never thought of it that way," said Dan. "Everything fits together so neatly. First, God made the world. Then came Man. Then the Garden. Then everything went wrong. The next thing you know, Joseph rescued the Jews who were starving in Egypt. Later Moses saved them a second time. He escaped them out of Egypt where they were in big trouble, trying to make bricks without straw, and a lot of other nearly impossible feats. God intercepted them on their flight route, handed down the Ten Commandments and beckoned them on their way. Centuries later, or two of them at least, they finally made it to the Promised Land, but not without some struggles. God was pulling the strings, but His "puppets" had to fight!"

THE ENSUING CONTEST
Prologue

Pray, be gentle with our fragile allegory.
Light-hearted? Yes. Frivolous? Never.
On tender ground walks he who would
Make light of a very serious business.
Five hundred pages, more than
One-third the depth of the Bible,
The heartbeat of revered and
Ancient Jewish history. Seventeen
Scriptures, Genesis through Esther.
Fifteen centuries. A monumental
Odyssey, tilling hallowed grounds,
Spawning and nourishing the seeds of Christianity.
In the Old Testament a contest of Olympian proportions
Played out.
The Old Testament was a vast playing field on which God
and Mankind meet in friendly contest.

* * * *

The Lord's determination was
"To make man in my image" and to keep him that way.
I think he also made the woman that way, too.

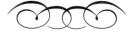

At first look it appears that God had set up an unfair game, that man has the odds stacked against him.

God is in control, to be sure.
He made the rules.
He rules the world.
He established the passing grades.
He is the referee.
He is the Boss.
He controls the game.
He decides when man is losing,
Or winning, which he (Man) usually doesn't —
Neither does the woman!

God is great; God is good.
Let us thank Him, for our game!

In a pragmatic and practical sense it is man himself who will be the winner or loser. Man is battling with his own strength and weaknesses, between what he is and what God wants him to become. God wants man to win. That's for sure. After all, He did not create His own image to be a loser.

In fact, in the final seconds of the contest, God personally joined the action and scored the winning goal for man, as it were. This event, two thousand years ahead of where we are now, is in embryo here. It took 2,000 years for the idea to gestate.

* * * *

As the contest is ready to start, God fields a line-up of his best, first-string players. Noah, Abraham, Isaac, Jacob, Joseph, Moses, Judge Samuel, King David, and David's son, "wrong way" Solomon, who got mixed up and ran over his own goal line, you might say. But then David did the same, too often. "Wrong Way Corrigans" are all over the Bible!

God blackboards his pre-game strategy in the early minutes of Genesis. Remember, in the First Chapter, God declared, "I will make man in my image, male and female," His edict is cathedral to the game's purpose. God's images will soon be on the field, never to leave, like players made in the image of the coach, or perhaps if you live in the New York area, the owner.

Around this challenge, the contest is played. God's people work the football up and down the field, sometimes scoring goals, more often than not being penalized for breaking the rules, fumbling often, dropping the ball, being intercepted, time and again, and botching a play or two on the one yard line!

Alert on the sidelines, God thinks up new plays to keep the tide surging towards his players' victory. The momentum of the "My Image" declaration is a current that courses through the entire Old Testament, controls its direction, frustrates its inept players, who catch on now and then but receive so little affirmation or support. Good God. Great Coach. He knew everything before Knute Rockne or Vince Lombardi. Even when you lose, winning is still everything.

Later, about 1800 or 2000 B.C., as one of his favorite players trotted on the field, God added two more elements to his original game plan: He instructed: "Go to a land that I will show you. Make a great nation. If you do as I ask, you will become a blessing to yourself, your people, and to all mankind." You (or they) will (finally) win the game. Abraham listened and became a blessing...Indeed.

Then came Moses to lead his people, down 48 to zero. After a long hiatus in the deserts of a foreign land, Moses appointed Joshua. Joshua snugged on his helmet, tightened his shoelaces, and without looking back, ran for the goal, no questions asked. "Those opposing tackles and linebackers look like 'giants!'," someone said. Joshua said, "I have the best interference in the world!"

Another element is a strategic concept. It is implied by God's deliberate insertion of the "Blessing" sentences. To Abraham He said: "I will bless you. You will be a blessing to mankind." With these announcements God hinted that he was holding in reserve a secret and special play, coded "Blessing," to rescue the game should his players fall apart. When all else fails, or is failing, and you are down and almost out, throw a "Hail Mary" pass, and someone will catch it!

It worked out, just about as God suspected it might. From time to time, His players dropped the ball and the Lord resorted to using His special "end around," "Statue of Liberty," hidden blessing plays. Finally, he whispered "Blessing" to his youngest star, His own Son, Jesus Christ, who crossed the goal line with a thrilling broken-field run and in what appeared to be a certain loss, He scored a crescendo victory, or rather through Him God did—and so did we.

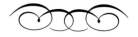

THE OLD TESTAMENT
(Some More)

For His own reasons God subtly nestled certain of His cherished operative declarations and decisions among seemingly routine and essentially innocuous statements. He wove a veiling shelter around His treasured ideas. When you suspect you have discovered the play book of your opponent, you treasure it. It awakens, there is movement, and sure enough it starts to wiggle with the secrets of the enemy's game. Satan seems to have full reign, but within the boundaries of what God allows. Ask Job. God knows and calls all His plays.

The Chief Event of The Old Testament

What is the chief event, Numero Uno, of the Old Testament? The New Testament's is simple—Jesus Christ: arrival, miracle, death, resurrection, Ascension, and waiting for his return. But the Old Testament, what's it about? People differ, even good people, great scholars. They do not agree. What are you and I to think?

Listen, balance, disagree, or decide. The choices are legion, i.e., many. Choice one: *Creation takes it all:* without the day it all began, nothing would have followed. Hands down. Thumbs up: Genesis 1:1 is salient, the greatest miracle of all, of all, of all. Out of no-thing, God made some-thing, the world, i.e., the universe. And all living creatures, too.

But, in choice two, there is the *"Blessing,"* given once and more to Abraham, the second Father of the human race. "You will be a blessing to all mankind," God said, and that's a great majestic saying. It is a rival for the Old Testament's major moment; once the world was here, we all sure need a blessing!

Then, there is *the Exodus.* Most good Jews (I mean religiously) would respond with ease: "The Number One event of the Old Testament is our Exodus, the wondrous day when our first born sons were spared their gift of life, by the Blood of the Lamb on the door post." All of Genesis is a kind of lengthy preparation, circuitous and unclear at times, to get God's people down to Egypt, at first to be rescued from famine—then from slavery.

If Genesis precedes it, all to come follows. The Prophets, Priests, Kings, and Holy people, keep reminding "If God was good enough to bring us out of Egypt, why are we faithless, and so full of doubt as to what our God, Jehovah, can do, will do, has done, is doing for His people?"

There are some others in the race for the chief event, but so far from the finish line they hardly need a mention: Like *King David,* more revered than Abraham, in the Holy Lands; like *Elijah* who had miraculous power, and was ascended directly into heaven while Elisha watched. In most books that would be the topper, but not here, even if Elijah had the tools for excellence and honor.

Some might finally say Ezra, Nehemiah, and *the return from Exile,* which but a few predicted, and which came against all odds. But Jerusalem was rebuilt, the temple back again, if not with its former splendor, but God filled the new one with His Splendor and His Peace.

The Old Testament has an endless revelation of all that God can do. It need not, should not, be ignored. It tells the noble story of a Creator God who loves and guides His people.

Chapter III
Let Us Begin

GENESIS

For example, the greatest miracle of all was the genesis of an idea: that a world could/would come to be. Out of nothing—ex-nihilo—God made something wonderful! Pretend you never heard these words before:

"In the beginning God created the heaven and the earth..." God said let there be light; and there was light. God called the dry land earth, and the gathering of the waters he called the seas. On the third day, God said let us divide the day from the night, and let there be seasons, and so forth....

Next God said, "Let us make man in our image, to have dominion over the fish of the sea and over the fowl of the air and over the beasts of the earth." And God blessed the man and the woman and told them to be fruitful, to multiply and to have dominion over every living thing that moveth, creepeth, flyeth, or swimmeth upon or above the earth, or under the water.

Then came the seventh day...After all that God needed a rest. He saw everything that He had made and behold it was very good!

> Thus the heavens and the earth were finished
> and all the host of them. And on the seventh
> day god ended his work and he rested on the
> seventh day from all his work which he had made.
> GENESIS 1:31

Without the initial proposal and its implicit challenge, the Bible Book would have no story line. There would be no plot, no problems to solve, no weaknesses to overcome, no successes to cheer. Its charge ignites a train of violent and explosive events. Come and see:

TIME TABLE OF THE BIBLE

So that we can grasp what is happening when, I have worked out this brief timetable. The following dates are estimates, arguable, not agreed by all. But they give an easy reference point. The times are almost never revealed within the Bible itself. One gets lost, confused, frustrated. But while my advisors differ, this will do:

4000 or 14 billion B.C.	God made the world.
4000 to 2000	God's people misbehaved, on one way or another (see Genesis 1–11).
1800's	God spurs Abraham and followers into Canaan. Son Isaac, Grandson Jacob succeed Abraham as leaders. The party roams the area for one hundred years.
1700's	Jacob's son Joseph settles starving clan in Egypt. Joseph is now Egypt's Premier and Head of State. Jews' sojourn in Egypt drags out to 400 years. Original camp of seventy souls swells to 1,000,000 Jews, more or less. Pressed into slavery. Corrupted. Bruised and battered.
1300's	Moses escapes them...via the Red Sea route and miracle. 50,0000–100,000 finally, after wandering in the wilderness, make camp in Jordan hills, overlooking Canaan. God hands down his Ten Commandments to Moses, who sees the Promised Land, but never gets there. Aaron and the people meanwhile were fashioning their golden calf.

1200's	Joshua, the successor to Moses, and his warriors. Eventually they occupy the land. They form tribal groups, governed by Judges.
1100's	Tribes establish Nation of Israel. Saul is first king, by demand of the people, by the anointing of Samuel.
1000's	Little Shepherd Boy David kills Goliath, a giant leader of common enemy, the Philistines. David anointed King by Judge Samuel, succeeding a sullied Saul. David moves capital to Jerusalem and dances with joy in the streets. David's son Solomon succeeds David as King. The kingdom rises to its zenith, but falls with King Solomon's greed and insatiable ego.
900's	Israel falls into civil war ... disintegrates ... North versus South. Covetous nations attack and loot Israel's fragments.
700's	Assyria decimates Israel's northern provinces. But watch it. The prophets are already there.
600's	Babylonia kidnaps southern Judah, ravages towns and villages, levels Jerusalem to the ground. Carries strong young men and beautiful young women to Babylon.

500's	Ezra and Nehemiah lead resettlement of empty, desolate Jewish lands, upon people's release from Babylonia. Israelites struggle to restore society, self-respect and dignity. They are variably successful. There are high points and low points marking their effort. The prophets warn of God's requirements, but like most warnings, never heeded.
300's to 200's	A renewed force led by Judas Maccabeaus, conquers the Holy Lands. By this time Alexander the Great's Greeks hold title to the property and the Temple. Hannukah begins here. (See Apocryphal Old Testament)
100's	Roman Empire forces invade, occupy, and dominate Palestine and the Jews. Install their own vassal kings, rulers, and procurators.
000	Jesus Christ emerges, survives a three-year ministry, dies at thirty-three. Rises once more, to glory.
50 A.D.	St. Paul travels with the Gospel to foreign lands.
70 A.D.	Romans clear Israel-Palestine of Jews, and Jerusalem is leveled once again. On the story goes . . .

TIME

A lot of things can happen in
Fourteen billion years, even four thousand
And four (Hello Bishop Usher!)
Like...the molten mass can cool,
The stars and planets find their
Courses, a tiny amoebic morsel feeds
Upon itself and pow, another miracle.
Life is here. Then more life,
Until God breathed His breath
And Adam was, and Eve,
Then Cain and Abel, the first two
Sons, had an awful fight.
Gone they were, Abel to Heaven,
Cain to East-of-Eden.
But life kept moving onward
And upward, until Enoch walked
With God. Methuselah lived to
Be Nine Hundred Seventy Three.
The gods came down to
Walk with men, or pardon, women.
Then mankind tried to build a
Tower up to heaven, God
Gave them babbling tongues;
And it all got worse.

So much so that God was
Sorry he had made His
Man and woman and He
Determined to flood them
All to kingdom some,
Except the fishes, large
And small. No one knows,
Or seems to care what happened
to the fishes, when the heavens
Poured their wrathful
Waters on the earth.
The ark creaked and rolled, and
Tossed in the terribly high
Seas, and came to rest
......Days later, on the
Tippy top of olde Mount Ararat!
Come down Noah.

HELLO NOAH!

"These people, like wayward children, are not grasping what I want for them. I must start all over," God said. And so, the Lord called upon Noah to build the ark, with no clouds in sight. Still, the rains came and the floods. Life was wiped out. Only Noah and his wife and their three sons and wives were saved, plus all the other animals and birds and the teeming other pairs aboard the ark, and of course some swimming fish.

Son Shem became an ancestor of Abraham, as well as all Jews, and Arabs, in the chain of people to follow. They are Semites of today. Noah's other sons did well, too, I think.

THE TIRELESS GIANT—ABRAHAM

Abraham & Sons
2,000 Years at This Location

The ancient holy lands of the Bible were a very special place of a very special time. They still are.

About the size of New Jersey, measuring two hundred miles long by fifty miles wide. Up and down the length of it they ranged. To cross and criss-cross.

God called out:
"THIS IS YOUR BIG DAY, ABRAHAM,
LET'S GET MOVING."

God and Abraham broke camp at dawn. They bruised their way overland battling hundreds of hard miles through cruel mountain country into the backlands of Canaan.

They were striding together side by side. Climbing a long, final hill they at last reached its crest. Abraham stopped. God's shoulder was almost touching his. Both looked into the distance. God turned to Abraham,

"We are here. You are home now. All land you can see...North, South, East and West I give to you and your descendants." (Genesis 13:15)

"You will build a great nation."

This is the scene of the famous Promised Land compact. These historical words are among God's first that bear directly on the turbulent events of the next two thousand years.

Beyond Abraham's Vision...

If Abraham could have seen
The trials and tests
the fears and failures
That lay ahead
For his distant millions
Of Jewish descendants,

He might well have had
Second thoughts.

He might well have
Hesitated...possibly even
Said, "No thanks."

God Talks to Abraham, Again

"I wonder if we are at last on the way," mused the Lord as He watched Abraham move into the distance toward his new Israel nation.

God had only recently concluded His initial command to Abraham, promising him success in the new venture and adding His Blessings. If God's promises cannot be trusted, can anybody else's?

As He paused looking after Abraham, God's mind drifted back into the past. He thought of His first try with Adam and Eve. It had ended in failure. "Only human," said God. "I cannot really blame them. I gave them free choice. I made it possible for them to taste the fruit of the Tree of Everlasting Life I warned them against. I could have prevented it, like puppets on a string. I could have pulled and pushed them about. I didn't."

Chapter IV
From Story to History!

(Genesis 12, and forward)

When they print a new edition of the Bible, they should insert several new, all-white pages between the end of Chapter 11, Genesis, and the beginning of Chapter 12, Genesis.

For Chapter 12 is the actual beginning of the 2,000 years of vibrant Jewish story, where God starts things moving.

The first eleven Genesis chapters cover creation of the world and chronicle the adventures of Adam and Eve, Noah, flood and ark. These stories are revered and famous, but we often call them pre-history.

But the starting-line of Old Testament, Hebrew Scripture action is actually Genesis 12, Verse 1. Abraham's native country, Chaldea (Babylonia) was in present-day Iraq and was a god-forsaken, pagan society of idol worshippers, successful indeed, but...going no place.

Even his father left Ur of the Chaldees, a generation earlier, up to Haran.

Sublime Proposition

A unique and sublime proposition unfolds
in the next few pages. It is so direct
and simple, at the same time so ripe
with shock waves, it is only prudent to
signal its approach in advance, like when
a Hurricane is on the way, you expect
the experts to tell you.

It is God's idea. Its effect turns the
world upside-down. Its momentum renews
itself, so that, gaining in strength, it
continues as a pulsing force throughout
the world today, 4,000 years after God
made the declaration.

You will find man seeking a haven of
spiritual sanctuary and repose. With
God's help he succeeds. The Jew finds
his God, or rather God found His people.

The Ten Commandments glow, then dim.
The nation flames, then sputters...
There is frustration and violence. God
steps in and pleads. The Jew listens and hears,
but apparently he does not understand.
Certainly he does not correct his ways.

Accordingly, God amends and supplements
His design. He goes all-out. He releases
His divine power at land level and establishes
direct, personal contact with His people.
He uses a human-body figure named Jesus
Christ as His Proxy.

Both schemes eventually prosper.

Jew and Christian, Abraham and Jesus.

"BLESSING"

In the opening lines of Jewish history God makes
a landmark declaration. It sets the stage for
2,000 years of tumultuous action.
The scene opens in the first verse of Genesis 12.
Abraham is being impelled to depart his native
homestead of ancient, pagan-worshipping lands
to search for a sanctuary of satisfying spiritual
reward. Abraham wants one God, his own God,
a God who will give him release and repose.
But God wants a man who wants One God, too.
The pagan-god, idol-worshipping syndrome of his
native country was an empty-headed, fruitless
and incoherent exercise for Abraham.

The Genesis 12 Declaration

In the first act of the drama, God is center stage. He declares:

> Abraham, leave your country.
> Leave these people behind you.
> Go to the land I will show you.

a) I will make you a great nation.
b) I will bless you.
c) I will make you important and famous.
d) You will be a blessing.
e) You will be a blessing to all mankind.[1]

> Abraham departs and arrives in Canaan.
> The Lord appears and says:

f) All this land I give you and your descendants.[2]

> Walk through all the land.
> The length and breadth of it.
> I give it unto thee.[3]

---

1. Genesis 12: 1,2,3
2. Genesis 12: 7
3. Genesis 13: 17

Note the "Blessing" Sentences

b) I will bless you.
d) You will be a blessing.
e) You will be a blessing to all mankind.

At face value these "blessing" lines are foreign to the land-and nation statements. You may omit them from the declaration without disturbing its sequitur, its rational thought-sequence. To wit,
Go to the land I will show you.

a) I will make you a great nation.
c) I will make you important.
f)   I give you all this land.
f)   Walk through it.

Two ideas are operating at once. A most unusual happening. God has carefully designed the presentation of His thought structure. This phenomenon is no careless-talk accident. God deliberately inserted the "blessing" messages among the land message.

A possible line of analysis is that God wants the land and the "blessing" to become spontaneously associated. For the moment land is tangible, "blessing" is intangible, although the latter condition could change later.

A thought-association process can also be identified in psychological terms as Conditioned Response. Witness the famous dog-and-bell experiment performed by Russian Dr. Pavlov.

Dog is given meat to eat. Dog salivates. Dog gets meat, eats, salivates...and Pavlov rings an electric bell. Meat, meat, mea...eat, eat, eat...salivate, salivate, salivate...bell, bell, bell. Repeat, repeat, repeat. At the end of the experiment Pavlov has the dog salivating when the bell alone rings. No meat...the dog salivates. Pavlov has taught the dog something new. Good dog.

"Land" and "blessing" become closely associated.

Symbolism. The current gift of land becomes a symbol representing God's love for man...and perhaps hints of more gifts to come. To such extent the land becomes ground "touched and blessed by God." By association it becomes a Holy Land, a land upon which, by definition, God has invoked divine favor.

With His use of the "blessing" technique God points toward a horizon well beyond immediate circumstances. Could His words refer to the future coming of Jesus Christ? Such an event is 2,000 years along the road, to be sure. But remember that God's powers are very special. Omnipotent. Omni-perceptive. Omni-prescient. A thousand years, after all, are but as a watch in the night.

There is one thing for sure that God's use of "blessing" is not. It is not a casual, colloquial use you sometimes hear today. "Have a good day, folks. Good-bye and God bless." This it is positively not. Blessing means: a special favor, granted by God.

Eulogy

Grasp this concept with your mind. It is your landmark.
The Bible story has many hills and valleys. Twists and turns.
Missteps and new steps. Should you become lost in the
maze, return home. Go back to the concept. It is your orient
point of the blueprint. Your puzzle will solve.

God said to the insides of Abraham:

> "You are tormented. Depart and
> follow my words. You need relief
> from the acidity of the dark side
> of human nature. I am your remedy.
> Together we will build My House.
> Then you shall dwell in it."

It was a long, long time, His House.
It has many parts—and pages—listed in
its Book of Specifications. It is easy
to get lost among them. Always return to
the beginning. It is your reference point, and mine.

> "You will be my blessing.
> I am your blessing."
> Both of us will benefit.

Chapter V
After Abraham and the Blessing
Isaac and Jacob

Exit Abraham, enter Isaac and Jacob. Another start, eons later. It is now 2000 or so B.C., possibly 1800. Abraham was sent away by God. His son Isaac, married, had two sons, Esau and Jacob. Jacob did his brother in. Stole the "Birthright," with his mother's help. Poor old Isaac, he didn't know what to do. "Too late," God whispered, "Jacob was my man, even if he was a mommy's boy, and a swindler! Isaac did not laugh.

In time Jacob had twelve sons, two of them by Rachel, his beloved, who died too young. The twelve became the leaders of the Tribes of Israel (Jacob's other name), but not yet.

Famine came and all would have starved to death had it not been for Rachel's older son. Israel and the boys went down to Egypt to find some food. Guess who gave it to them....

JOSEPH, THE POINT MAN

A bright fourteen year old boy, Joseph, son of Jacob is about to become "a second father of his country." But he and the Jews do not know it yet. Little Joe, who wound up as a foreign Premier of all Egypt, unheard of, begins his career in jail. His jealous brothers had booted him out of Canaan, sold him to a passing traders' caravan, Midianites, and told his father he was dead.

Joseph is a combination dreamer and doer. A "B" type and an "A" type, two-facet personality. The guys in jail with him had bad dreams. Joseph interpreted the meaning and gave his mates answers they liked to hear. One of them happened to be a Pharaoh kitchen chef, who had got caught with his finger in the Pharaoh's cookie jar.

The Pharaoh, also dream-troubled, invited Joseph to join the household as an aide, if he could correctly interpret the Pharaoh's dream. In a short time, he gained the Pharaoh's ear on all matters, including nightmares. Soon Joseph's advice is heeded by inner circle court politicians.

The Pharaoh had a dream which forecast a devastating famine ahead. Joseph advised that they gather a lot of food. Responding, the Egyptians lay in huge stockpiles of corn, wheat and grain. Sure enough the famine came. They were ready, thanks to Joseph.

Responding to a plea from his starving Canaan brothers, Joseph arranged for seventy Jewish refugees, his relatives, to enter Egypt for safety and something to eat. These folks not only stayed for a weekend, they liked the place so much they settled in for a couple of hundred years. God knew all the while.

You might say Joseph's talent was "The Dream that Launched a Million Jews."

DOMINOES

The sequence of events which punctuate God's successful rescue plan fall into place with uncanny accuracy. Its synchronized pattern reminds you of a game sometimes played with dominoes. You stand them up on one end in a line one after the other. Steady now...

Push No. 1. It tips forward and pushes No. 2. Two falls and trips No. 3. It is fun and fascinating. All the way down to the end of the line. Each piece falls just where you want it. One guy used to do it on TV—10,000 dominoes all fell down in sequence.

Domino No. 1   is Joseph.
      No. 2   is a famine.
      No. 3   is Joseph again, at the right place at the right time with the right power in Egypt.
      No. 4   is a storehouse of food.
      No. 5   is pride, which Joseph's "bad" Canaan brothers swallow. They come to ask him for help.
      No. 6   is forgiveness warming within Joseph.
      No. 7   is sanctuary in Egypt for Joseph's family.
      No. 8   is God's Breath of Life. Seventy Jews grow to 1,000,000 souls.
      No. 9   This domino wobbles. Many of the multitude of Jews fall out of line, into crime and slavery.
      No. 10 a young Pharaoh lady discovers a hidden Jewish baby.
      No. 11 The baby turns out to be Moses.
      No. 12 Moses leads Abraham's "family" to safety and to the "Land of Promise."

One domino follows another. Each falls neatly in its preselected place. Who put them there? Who fixed them that way? God, of course.

Why pick Joseph in the first place to go to Egypt? Why sell him as a slave? Why not some other Jewish lad? Because he is the son of Jacob, who is the son of Isaac, who is the son of Abraham? You can show a direct and traceable bloodline. It guarantees purity of breed. Thoroughbreds. The line goes straight back to Abraham and God. Impeccable and faultless integrity. Check the geneology of Jesus, The Christ.

The purpose *of outlining* the series of events is to help you see them with clarity. They are links of a chain. If any one of the links had failed, the sequence would be broken. The plan would fail. Coincidence would have taken over once again.

For example:

If Joseph had been a dumbell, a respondent rather than a self-starter, the plan would fail at its outset.

If there had been no famine, there would be no need for action. No motivation.

If there had been no storehouses of food, there would have been no lure, no bait. No incentive.

If there had been no dreams followed by acceptable interpretations, Joseph would not have caught the Pharaoh's ear nor would food have been gathered. No answer.

The Canaan brothers could have procrastinated and voted "No." But they said "Yes" and went to Joseph for help.

Joseph could have turned them away. He did not.

Later, Moses, a hidden Jewish baby, was miraculously discovered and saved. And this followed a pharaoh order that all Jewish infants be tracked down and killed.

Does this sequence of events fall beyond the laws of chance? A heads or tails flip of a coin? Are the odds better than a 50-50 proposition?

You decide. You figure it. Each of the options had to come up heads to insure success. Or, negatively, a failure of any one would have closed out the story.

The real-life facts say this scenario was planned and guided by the steady hand of a gifted Master Craftsman.

One of the big stories of the Bible —
Seldom noted as such.

Chapter VI
Moses and the Law

When you move from the end of Genesis to Chapter One of Exodus, be careful; two hundred years at least have passed. We left the chosen people down in Egypt with Prime Minister Joseph, the leader of the band. But watch how subtly the author says it "now there arose a new king in Egypt who did not know Joseph." Wham! That's enough of these foreigners over here hogging up all the good jobs, trading for their own good with our money. The new king seems to have said, "I will cut them down to size!" And he did...for a while. Made their lot so miserable they could have died, trying to make bricks without straw.

One young Jew, born and saved in peculiar bullrushes, became so angry with the guards' treatment of his people he killed an Egyptian guard and fled for his dear life. He made it.

Then one day, after he had married and had two sons, he was out in the pleasant fields of his father-in-law, when a bush caught fire and he heard the voice of God telling him to go back to Egypt. He, with a price on his head, refused and began to make excuses. God would have none of it. Moses went. And, as you know, "The bush was not consumed."

Then God brought the plagues: "Oh Pharaoh, why don't you listen and let my people go?" He finally did but not until the last one, when the first born son of every Egyptian in the land died on the same night, which proves God doesn't fool around.

Only with the blood of the lamb painted on their doorways, the sons of the Israelites were spared. What a God! Pass-over.

So off they went. The Red Sea opened for them and closed on the Egyptians. They went down to Mount Sinai, grumbling all the way. At one point they even wanted to go back to the degradation of slavery, rather than wander with God in the wilderness.

On the mountain Moses was given the laws of God while they played with a golden calf down in the valley. Moses was furious of course.

But they finally made it to the Jordan River, a whole generation later where on top of Mount Nebo, on the Jordanian side of the river, Moses saw over into the promised land, but he never got there for he died.

MOSES, BY HIMSELF...

God moves His men and women onto stage whenever He has need of them. Mostly they are good actors, at least they play their parts, sometimes good, often great, sometimes poor, at times horrible and the heavens boo!

Just prior to the time of entry into the Promised Land, two hundred years before Solomon, Doctor Moses delivered his staff's conclusions to the patient:

> "If you do not strictly adhere to this regimen, the Curse of God will be upon you. All but a handful of you will die.
>
> "We have observed you most carefully, O people of Israel. We have processed you thru our full battery of tests. The results remain questionable.
>
> "I repeat. The Curse of God will be upon anyone, who:
>
> 1. "Worships an idol, even in secret, whether made of wood or metal. Such handmade gods are hated by the Lord.
> 2. "Commits adultery with one of his father's wives.
> 3. "Takes advantage of a blind man.
> 4. "Has sexual intercourse with an animal. (Ugh!)

5. "Moves a boundary marker between his land and his neighbor's.
6. "Has sexual intercourse with his sister, (whether she be a full sister or a half-sister) "...No sister-in-law...?
7. "Secretly slays another.
8. "Has sexual intercourse with his mother-in-law."

(DEUTERONOMY 27:15 - 25
and 28:20 - 21)

Moses Displays a Nagging Uneasiness...
"No more whooping it up with mother-in-law."
"No more hanky-panky with sheep in the hay."
Perhaps he also had a distressing premonition of the pains which lay beyond. His face was grim and his lips drawn tight as he posted his bulletin. He felt sick to his stomach, the doctor did.

The patience of his God was being sorely tried.

Moses' riveting lines were an indictment of "Christmas present" and an estimate of "Christmas to come."

Primitive, tribal times. Nature in-the-raw on the loose. Gorging, pressing earthy drives.

Scrambling suburbia, USA...and all points elsewhere.

Same world all-over.

They all live just down the street.

LAW VERSUS LOVE

As Moses led them out, the Jews had been in Egypt a couple of hundred years. To keep this length of time in perspective, note that the United States of America today is just a little over two hundred years old.

Moses' people sloshed their way through the swampy Sea of Reeds and reached dry land beyond Egypt. (They did not traverse the Red Sea as romantic conception depicts the scene.) It was mountainous, rough and dry country. They moved eastwards and 'up,' toward today's Jordan area, keeping Canaan-Palestine-Israel lands to their left. (Some wits observe that if they had only turned right, they might have struck oil in Saudi Arabia.)

Not many days out they halted at Mount Horeb (Mount Sinai) where they found drinking water. Moses had a 'call' from God. He climbed the mount alone. God gave him the Ten Commandments.

You may identify these rules as "commands," or what you will—suggestions...advisories...warnings...guidelines. They expressed a code for living. A series of standards against which the Jews could measure their conduct.

Jewish leadership characterized them as "The Law," or "Laws." The Commandments became the stimulus for and the basis of hundreds of future decrees: laws and regulations composed by high priests.

Jewish priesthood hierarchy, totally preoccupied with 'laws' devised another six hundred to add to God's original Ten. The decrees covered all aspects of living to a brain-busting limit.

Personal and intimate orders regulating haircuts, circumcision, tatooing skin and forbidden foods (no eating cloven-hoofed animals that did not chew a cud) to planting trees in specified locations. General and civic laws like no marriage to 'aliens,' no lighting of cooking fires on the Sabbath, and laws of inheritance (the first son got a double share of the estate). The Laws are detailed in Bible books Leviticus, Numbers and Deuteronomy.

Priests had grabbed the Law idea and run with it. They squeezed the everyday Jew with strictures. 'Laws' had the populace looking over its shoulder in anxiety. They became a nerve-wracking burden.

The Burden

The everyday person's feelings of restriction and frustration arose from worry about breaking the Law, and, therefore, not 'making it' in the eyes of God.

Interestingly, and curiously, the original Ten Commandments do not contain an 'escape clause.' There is no allowance nor margin for error. If you broke the Law, you became a failure in God's Judgment. No wonder Paul commented and complained about "The Burden" in later times. And therewith pointed in the direction of Jesus.

Comment: The awareness of an omission of an 'escape clause' is an overwhelming discovery.

It will be helpful to jump ahead some hundreds of years to see the net effect 'Law' activity had on men and women of the times and, additionally, on Judaism as a religion.

Looking 'way up front,' Jesus came.

From Him, love, faith and forgiveness.

With such a happening at hand you have, travelling side by side, two approaches to religion and God. One, the Law. The other, Love.

Each is solid and enduring in its own right.

Seeking relief from frustration and anxiety could well explain why Israelites flocked to hear John the Baptist and Jesus, and be near the Lord.

4,000 and 5,000 massed more than once to be with Him. They came out of the woodwork when they heard He was in the neighborhood.

You know now that Jesus Christ reinforced His positions and promises with tangible evidence. Explosively demonstrated with His dying body thrashing on His Cross. Soon followed by His promised physical Reappearance. Not once, but three times, and more!!

It is curious that—and why—the priesthood did not pick up God's earlier words to Abraham, "I will bless you." Perhaps they did not understand. Or, did they choose not to pursue. The priest hierarchy was a controlling force holding overtones of political power in very early times.

Whatever, they devoted their energies to Laws. Writing, re-writing. They concentrated on their own chosen mission. God was their discovery. They would hold God, as their own. They did not "Pass the word," as God had asked.

Which conflict turned out all right. God has His own answer. He came to His people in the Presence of Jesus. Relatively speaking, Christianity swept the world. Why? How come?

Jesus' actions were more imaginative and exciting than the priesthood approach. Jesus offered challenge and hope to the individual.

You can express this thought in a number of ways. Christ's words and actions were extroverted. Fluid. Fluent. They were the words of a salesman, persuasively couched, to tap the human nature of a human being. The Judaism priests' approach, by contrast was relatively introverted... introspective. Rigid. Stiff. Dead, or dying.

Jewish religious hierarchy concentrated on pen and scroll. It wrote Laws. Christianity aimed its energies at the person, his and hers hopes and fears, offering salvation and forgiveness.

TEN COMMANDMENTS

The Lord kept trying to get His people headed right. There came the Commandments, hundreds of them, by actual count, but Ten essential ones for man to follow.

With Abraham's people Yahweh (the other name then for God) had a fresh start. They were not all bad, I hope. This time He added a charted course. He handed Moses the Ten Commandments, a list of specifications against which the people should measure their behavior and conduct. Four commandments addressed religious matters; the six other spoke to everyday moral and social codes, using the famous "Thou Shalt Not" admonition as a salutation. A negative rather than positive and inspiring approach. Moses did not get to go to a Dale Carnegie course.

The thing did not work out: God gave it a 700-year try, but the people never did figure it out or grasp the ultimate purpose.

In fact, it may rest as an open question that the charted rules may not have been clear enough to show the people His true course and goal. Or, whose fault was it: The Commandments, Man's, or God's? If given a choice like that, always answer Man's.

But still, as noted, the problem was that there was no "escape clause," no forgiveness, included among the original Ten Commandments, nor suggested later by the ruling priest clique, the moral leaders who managed the Jews' religious life. In fact the priests compounded and confused by adding six hundred or more laws of their own design, some of which were frankly silly and self-serving.

But, in light of subsequent events, it is evident that lack of an "escape clause" was a serious omission, intentional or otherwise. For example, if you did something that "broke the law," there was no way to say, "I am sorry. I made a mistake. Please forgive me." The guilt festered as a hostile adversary in your mind. Ever present. No escape. No relief. For the rest of your living days and nights, it was there. Paul complains bitterly about this problem in his New Testament letters. Paul uses the word "burden." Guilt is a burden. So is feeling guilty.

When you contemplate the stress-load such a condition could cause upon a soul or psyche, your conjectures will appall you. You freeze up. You react as a robot. You do things as a duty, without compassion and warmth. And, you wonder out loud and in silence.

Secondly, another condition accompanies the Commandments' scheme. It was implicit and understood that if you broke one law, you broke them all. If you fibbed, or stole a single pair of sandals, you were just as guilty as having committed adultery or murder—no room to maneuver. You could not resort to a District Attorney plea-bargain deal, no temporary insanity plea. Guilty! Break one law and you were up to your neck in trouble. If this is not a dead-end impasse, nothing is. Jesus Christ's brother James refers to the "break one, break all" situation in his New Testament book (James 2). Also Galatians 3:10, by Paul; and way back in Deuteronomy 27:26.

Some of the Jews of the "Commandments" period remained loyal to their God, honoring holy days and making the required sacrificial devotions on the Sabbath, as God had commanded. But, as well, there were many others who "slipped" and returned to worship "foreign" deities.

In any event, the nation disintegrated not only as a political entity, but equally critically, the people moldered morally. Abraham's family was in tatters and disarray.

The Ten Commandments "Thou Shalt Not" Laws did not stimulate positive emotional response. You might say they pushed and shoved rather than inspired fulfillment and hope of reward. The futility of the conflict between the basic drives of human nature and acknowledging the laws only as a response to a sense of duty must have been amply evident to the Lord. He surely saw that His plan and design were going no place. No disrespect intended to The Commandments!

Goodbye Moses, who died atop Mt. Nebo, looking over into the Promised Land, but he never got to go, and no one knows where he is (was) buried—to this day. And, you can be sure the tourguides of Palestine would show you—if they knew...

Chapter VII
Joshua and the Promised Land

Joshua, the successor chosen by Moses, was brave, strong, confident, and holy. He became mighty when God told him to take over for Moses and to lead the people home!

Soon after they crossed the stream, the River Jordan, at a spot near where a young man named Jesus would be baptized twelve hundred years later, the Jews, under Joshua, initiated moves to establish an orderly society, as opposed to their habitual, primitive tribal customs.

The Promised Land

The Jews wanted the coastal shores badly. They needed the Promised Land to keep the story going, or rather God needed them to be there. Promised Land…"It's ours…then why are all those foreigners there already, some as huge as giants?"

"Well," said God, "I never said it would be easy. Lots of lands are promised, but you have to fight to get them." The other team will not just fall down and let you cross their goal line. Now, will they? It's fourth down and two to go, the toughest part of the field!

Philistines … Palestine

The most familiar of the adversaries, who hardened into enemies, is represented by the word Palestinians. The word Palestine derives from Philistia. The Philistines were "bad guys." Even as recently as 1900 in America you could disparage someone nasty as, "He's a Philistine." Or, you could still call your enemy football team, instead of bums or sluggards, "the Philistines!"

Historians say the Philistines originally had been booted out of the Island of Crete, nearby in the Mediterranean Sea, and in their small boats had sailed to escape to the seashore coastline of Canaan, today's Israel.

So the Jews conquered Philistia, which derives to Palestine, seen often in today's newsprint. The Palestinians would know what it means, today. So would the Israelies.

HERE COME THE JUDGES!

When Moses and Joshua were gone the way of all flesh, the time came for the Judges, a group of marvelous men and a woman. There were nine Judges, the way I count them. Most of them were good, at least they were most of the time. Some of them were entirely unknown by name to me. The people were the problem. They "did what was right in their own eyes," a comment frequently repeated in the Judges' book.

When all went wrong, the people stumbled and fell time and time again. So, "then the Lord raised up a Judge, who saved them out of the power of those who plundered them" (Judges 2:16) "and yet, they did not listen to their Judges...they soon turned aside from the way in which their fathers had walked..." (Is anything ever new?)

Speaking of Judges: did you ever hear of EHUD? He was one of the first Judges (Judges 3). His assault against Eglon, King of Moab, will engross you, to say nothing of what Jael did to entice Sisera to his death. The Bible is not always a gentle book!

Barak was another Judge. Gideon was too, and he was fine and pure and strong. Good leader, God loving. Then there were Jephthah and Jair, who had thirty sons, and others.

But, surprise, one of the ruling Judges, Man of God, was a woman. *Deborah* was a prophet, priest, warrior, woman. (See Judges 4) Great reading this and we have not yet mentioned Samson, who was not the equal of Deborah, not according to the Bible.

SAMSON

"Judge" Samson tied the tails of skittery foxes together, one to another, set the tails afire and whacked the flaming foxes scampering through lush Philistine wheat fields, just as red American Indians shot flaming arrows into the roofs of white American blockhouse structures.

The little foxes, with their flaming tails chasing them, set the wheat fields ablaze. What a picture...

Samson indulged in some girl-fun. He romanced a bunch, then a Philistine girl, Delilah, on the sly. One day she found his weakness—and his strength. That's the way it always is. Samson's wiles and Delilah's charms finished him. Samson, bound and blind in a Philistine temple headquarters, pushed the building down, column by column, monolith by monolith. Most graphic. Jewish folklore has Samson about nine feet tall and weighing in at four hundred muscle pounds.

The Judges tried hard. Still the people did not listen. Their devotion to God, ordered by the Ten Commandments, was generally slip-shod and half-hearted, if not downright irreverent. They still kept on...and did what was right in their own eyes. And, God does not ever cotton to that!

The Jews were headed for a big tumble.

Moral and spiritual disintegration had become rooted. God had reached His limit and had come to a decision. The time of the Judges was over. He yielded and gave the people a king, just like all their neighbors had...even if *He* did not want to. Sometimes you have to give your children what they want—not you (right?) even if it's wrong!

Chapter VIII
The Kings

So when the Judges left, Samuel came, at their request, and found them a king. The first was Saul. The people demanded that Samuel find them a King, like the other fellows in the neighborhood. God did not seem to want a King. Saul was tall and wonderful, for a while. But he had fits of temper, went insane, and finally killed himself with his own sword. (Several books and chapters of scripture have gone by.)

Then God said, "If they want a King, I will get them a good one: Samuel, go get David, the little shepherd boy." King David of the Nation of Israel was the man who eventually conquered the territory. A young sheep-keeper who played the harp and carried a slingshot as a sidearm in his holster: undaunted, David challenged a top general of the Philistine armed forces, Goliath. He zapped the general with a stone to the forehead, stole his sword which he kept forever. David was on his way to succeed Saul as King of Israel, even if Saul did not appreciate it.

But David was not perfect—far from it. While he was King, he ordered a top soldier to the front battle lines to be killed. He thereby had a clear path to the soldier's lady, to whom he was charming. Later David sorely repented and it is recorded that God forgave him.

Travelers to Israel today say the contemporary Jews' Number One Man clearly is King David: America's George Washington, Father of his country. Or is he more like Lincoln, if Abraham is the first father?

SOLOMON STRIKES GOLD

Then came Solomon, David's Son
in
I Kings 10:10
II Chronicles 9:14

1000's B.C.:

"Each year King Solomon received twenty-five tons of gold." (At a 1990 rate of $400 per ounce, that equals $320,000,000 annually.)

"He had some of the gold beaten into three hundred shields and pieces of armor for his palace guard."

"He had made a huge throne of pure ivory and overlaid it with pure gold."

"Once every three years his merchant fleet arrived with huge cargos of gold, silver, ivory, apes, and peacocks."

"He had a great stable of horses with a vast number of chariots and cavalry. There were fourteen hundred chariots in all and twelve thousand cavalrymen who lived in chariot cities and with him in Jerusalem," and they all were Solomon's men.

* * * *

A book of commentary offers that Solomon's weekend fluff, the Queen of Sheba, did a double-take when she first laid eyes on the solid gold fixtures in his palace bathrooms.

But, eventually they Rolled Him Away
In His Golden Wheelchair
Goodbye, Solomon.

King Solomon was a symptom of the disease, not the cause.

As a clean, young man he was off to a flying start. To his father, King David, the Lord God had said, "I give you a son who will be a man of peace. His name will be Solomon. He will build my temple. He shall be as my son. "I will be his father." (I Chronicles 22:9, 10)

The incoming Jews, led by Joshua, had mixed with the settled, incumbent Canaanites. It was a doomed, sickening combination. The Canaanites were heathens: pagans who worshipped an ugly artificial idol called Baal. Whatever religious and moral fibre the Jews carried with them was soon diluted and lost in their earthly struggles for survival and pursuit of passions. They even had prostitutes waiting at the temple. The sounds of God's Ten Commandments dimmed.

Solomon built the glorious Holy Temple he had promised the Lord. And then slapped God in the face, so to speak, by placing heathen altars for pagan sacrifices to Baal alongside it.

He pressed the everyday man into slavery and built himself a magnificent showplace of a palace, which he promptly loaded with seven hundred wives and three hundred concubines, monitored by a staff of eunuchs, all faithful to Solomon. Wow!

Solomon went madly and completely haywire. Bananas! You will have to read between the lines on this one. Morals went bad. Religion went bad. Everything went bad. But it was forced slavery and back-breaking taxes that triggered open revolution.

The ten northern tribes (Israel) split from the two southern (Judah, including Jerusalem). The divided Nation would now be viciously attached by foreign entities.

CATASTROPHE

Shades of Abraham.

From an aimless, wandering, desert tribe
To resounding, glorifying acclaim.
The world looked with awe upon
King Solomon's golden showcase.

But it was more than a lavish extravaganza.

It was — gross and blatant.
Stuff that feeds an insatiable ego.
An alluring, gleaming bait.
Certain to catch a covetous eye.

It was a symptom of terminal illness.
It spreads, it eats, it chokes.
It caught up with Solomon. He loved it,
And it ate him alive.

A cancer.

Is anything new under the sun?

After Solomon:
NATION SPLITS
WAR
NORTH VS. SOUTH
(A Civil War)

Swooping vultures:
Egypt, Assyria, Babylon
hungrily eyed the
wounded, struggling prey.
They plotted and descended.

They would set in motion
the most cataclysmic series of
centuries ever endured by man.

EGYPT MAKES THE FIRST STRIKE

900'S B.C. Egypt Plunders

Target Jerusalem...Pharaoh Sheshouk attacks with vast armies...wastes seventy communities...loots center city Jerusalem...strikes gold. A Blitzkrieg operation, like Hitler's plunge through Poland, Holland, Belgium and France. Temples and palaces robbed...gold, gems...vast treasures are swept up and carried away.

But it was a one-time shot. They beat it back to Egypt, leaving scorched earth in their wake.

Sheshouk's body was found in AD 1939, encased in sheets of solid gold. Possibly some of Solomon's palace guard shields, hammered flat, had finally come to the surface.

* * * *

Protracted Emergency Foreseen

MULTI-CHAIN COLLISIONS SHUT DOWN ISRAELITE HIGHWAY

PROPHETS ARE RUSHED TO SCENE

Two things were happening at once.
1. Jews were fighting for their lives.
2. God was punishing them and saving them at the same time.

God called up the Prophets to be His spokesmen to help in the emergency. This was a period of extreme stress for both God and His people, from the 900's B.C. through the 500's B.C.

The Prophets were specially selected by God. Their words were God's Word. Their passages frequently began with *"The Lord Saith."* Read them as being set in quotes... "Saith," by the way, is pronounced more like "seth."

There are three hundred pages of Prophet writings, comprising twenty-five percent of the Bible's contents, about as long as the entire New Testament. Sixteen men recorded seventeen books. Jeremiah wrote his own, and Lamentations.

An everyday person has a most limited perception and understanding of the part Prophets play in the Bible story. Isaiah is probably the best known name.

GOD CLEANS HOUSE #1

700's B.C. Assyria Annihilates
The Northern Division (Israel) was literally wiped from the face of the earth. Over a period of fifty years Assyrian soldiers swept the communities clean and clear. Thousands upon thousands of Jewish people disappeared. Carried away and never heard of again. All ten tribes of the original Jewish

twelve vanished. The two tribes of the Southern Division (Judah) were not touched...not yet.

Assyria was about three hundred miles north and east of Babylon on the Tigris River. Assyrians were an insanely brutal people. Skinned captives alive...tore out tongues... gouged out eyes, young girls and young mothers gone! Their empire, which traced back to Abraham times, disintegrated and disappeared soon after the rampage of Israel.

* * * *

600's B.C. Babylon Kidnaps

Ruthless Babylon warriors smashed the two remaining Israel tribes—the Southern Division (Judah)—and literally lashed them herd-like back to Babylon. Seventy-five thousand Israel men, women and children were in the round-up for the five-hundred mile trip. A journey the distance of New York to Detroit.

They looted the temples and palaces of Jerusalem and levelled the buildings to smashed piles of crumbled stone. The land lay empty and desolate for sixty years or so, as the Jews would find it when they returned from Babylonia about 550 B.C.

THE PROPHETS

So presumptuous it would
Be, of me, or anybody,
To try to introduce the prophets.
I have read (or seen)
Three dozen books at least,
Scholars most,
Who dissect each one,
And in their need,
Destroyed the unanimity
Of each. I mean
Literally dissect and destroy.
That is to say, I
Have been so confounded
And confused by
Those who have their own
Tale to tell, of
How Isaiah was written
By three or was it
Thirteen different men.

The only thing they all
Agree upon is that
No woman ever wrote
A thirteenth part.
I think its easier,
Except for a very
Few exceptions,
To land down where the
Ancients did and read
Them all as one.

I suppose there were
Two or three "Isaiahs."
There probably never was
A Jonah. The extravagant
Feats of Elijah and Elusha
(The earlier prophets)
Too often overlap,
And hence, suspicion and
A touch of incredulity.

True...
But then you can also nit-
Pick Moses and the Pentateuch
To death to say nothing
Of the miracles of Jesus or
The latter New Testament
Letters. It's good to
Know as much as
You can know. I know,
But if you miss the forest
Citing the imperfections of
The trees, you have
Missed it all, or all
Except the tree you're
Looking at.

Karl Barth, a finer
Modern theologian than
All these scholars put
Together (I am told),
Advised that what
We still had to do
Was "Read the Bible!"
Period, over and out!
The Word of God is
There. Try it and see.

Billy Graham
Once added, "It was
When I quit defending
The Bible and started
Preaching it, that
My gospel came
Together. And the
People finally began
To listen.

So, Lord, do you have a prophet? "Yes."

* * * *

MICAH, A PROPHET

Micah is one of the sixteen prophets whose book is recorded in the Old Testament. The passages on the following three pages reflect the essence of Micah's writings...

MICAH is one of the shorter prophet scripts.

It sounds all the tones which scholars agree characterize the message of the prophets.

It promises terror and punishment.

It softens and suggests hope.

It forecasts the coming of a King, a saviour.

Isaiah, Jeremiah and Ezekiel are the major prophets, but Micah is my favorite.

* * * *

Historians date Micah about 750 B.C.

This estimate puts him concurrently alongside, or just prior to, the Assyrian attack on Israel.

...About seven hundred years before the coming of Jesus Christ.

MICAH'S VOICE Is the Breath of God

Micah's talk is blunt and direct.
He calls it as he sees it.

Except that this is not Micah talking
It is God, Micah said.

If you can make this mental exchange
In your perception,
You have found
Another new discovery.

You are face to face
with the actuality of God.

The reality of God talking like Man.
Micah's candid words are today's straight-talk.
This revelation-experience
Happens throughout the Bible
When you find the right passages.

FAMOUS VERSE
(Often Quoted for Sunday Services)

"This is all God wants of you.
"Be fair to others.
"Conduct yourself justly.
"Behave with mercy.
"Show compassion upon others.
"Walk humbly with your God.
"Show reverence for your God."

MICAH 6:8 (RSV)

It is John language.
It is Paul talk.
It could be a quote out of Jesus Christ Himself.
In fact, it is just that.

EXILE

Then, God swept into the northern Israeli-Jewish settlements, wiping the lands clean. The enemies, selected by God, were violent, merciless warriors. The attackers scoured the southern settlements, Judah and its capital, Jerusalem. The Jews were herded into exile, their temples, palaces and lands devastated. They would not be released from Babylonia to return to their homelands for three generations, sixty-seventy years. They sat down by the river over there and wept, homesick for Jerusalem.

While they were there, many remained faithful. Like Daniel calmed the hungry lions in their den, dropped there because he refused to turn his back on home.

Shadrach, Meshach, and Abednego were hurled into a fiery furnace for their faith, and danced with an angel in the roaring flames. Some God!

Chapter IX
The Return from Exile:
The Persevering Jews

As in the flood situation, God had carefully provided that enough Jews, "a remnant," would survive the Babylonian exile to return, recover and revive their homeland. The well-known Biblical Nehemiah and Ezra pioneered this effort to tangible results.

These new Jewish "pilgrims" multiplied and survived for another 400/500 years, but never regained the zest, homogeneity and strength they had enjoyed under the reign of Kings David and Solomon. They were broken as a viable force.

Some new powers loomed on the horizon and God saw them coming. First the Greeks and then the Roman Empire. We are talking about centuries. They would devour the Jews and snatch their homeland away, again and again and again —in fact all the way to the end of World War II.

The Lord decided to move, in the fullness of time. As He had promised, as Moses had confirmed, "I (God) will raise up a Prophet. I will put my words in his mouth" (Deuteronomy 18:15–18), and as His Prophets later affirmed, a Saviour would come, to be born in Bethlehem, who would save the people from their sins.

HOME IS THE HEARTH

The Hebrew Holy Scriptures
are the Hearth and Home
of Jewish devotion.

They are impressed in print,
As carved in stone.

For centuries past, present
And beyond to ponder.

And wonder.

The TORAH is the heartbeat.

The Holy Scriptures are the hearth.

THE PERPETUAL JEW
He Saw Them All and Beat Them All

"Sound, Splendor and Dreamstuff..."

"The Egyptian, the Assyrian and the Babylonian rose, filled the planet with sound and splendor, then faded to dreamstuff and passed away. The Greek and the Roman followed and made a vast noise, and they are gone. Other peoples have sprung up and held their torch high for a time. But it too burned out and they sit in the twilight now or have vanished.

The Jew saw them all, beat them all, and now is as he always was, exhibiting no decadence, no infirmities of age, no weakening of his parts, no slowing of his energies, no dulling of his alert and aggressive mind.

All things are mortal but the Jew: all other forces pass, but he remains.

What is the secret of his immortality?"

The Secret of
THE INSCRUTABLE JEW

A Jew's beliefs
are locked in his head
where nobody can get at them.

That is why
He has endured and survived
When many others
Have withered and died.

Chapter X
"A Recapitulation"

Mark Twain. *Harper's Magazine*
September, 1899

The main events of the Old Testament are accounts of the flow and ebb of God's attempts to achieve His goal. . .that mankind be made as a reflection of Him. "I will make man in my own image," He says in Genesis 1:27. This statement says, in effect, "I want man to be a reflection of me on earth. I want to communicate with him, and have him communicate with me. I want to help him help me. I want to be his God, but also to be his friend."

God made many attempts to reach His goal. We said four earlier, now it must be stretched to seven. Man failed each time...(1) The first was Adam and Eve. According to the Beginning Book, it all began in a Garden:

> The Lord planted a garden in Eden, in the east; and there He put the man whom He had formed." (Genesis 2:8) It was a pleasant place to be, a place of peace. This Garden was God's first gift to man, except of course the Gift of Life. Eve was there, too, at the beginning: "Male and female created He them."

Everything they needed or wanted was there, free for nothing. They could do anything and everything save one thing. No one knows for sure what "it" was. The story calls it, "The Tree of the Knowledge of Good and Evil," which they were not to touch. They did. You know the rest of the story. They failed...to temptation. God therewith chased them out of the Garden. Eden was gone—for good.

Secondly, following Adam and Eve, God brought thousands of people. These masses also fail His intended purpose. They try to be like God. They sin shamelessly. He drowns them in a deep, wet flood.

Thirdly, starting anew with Noah and his descendants, then in time Abraham, God generates a whole new population. Here, The Lord activated a proposition which is key. (Don't miss this one!) "Abraham, your "family" will be a blessing to all mankind. I will bless you. And you, in turn, will be a blessing to me and to all the peoples of the earth."

The BLESSING DECLARATION, in Genesis Twelve, analyzes the Lord's prescient use of a code word, "Blessing," in His send-off remarks to Abraham. The study suggests—and documents with quotes from Moses (O.T.) and Saint Paul (N.T.)—that with "Blessing" God may well have been implying, two thousand years in advance, that an event of remarkable proportions lay ahead for mankind. Observations on this possibility appear from time to time in the Old Testament; and, of course, in the New.

Abraham journeyed well. He did just about exactly what God wanted. He was willing to sacrifice his only son, Isaac. Is that another pursuant parallel, which will touch the sacrifice of an only son much later on? It seems so. Abraham and God were close, as slave and master, but close enough to be called friends. Many people love their slaves and their masters!

Abraham was not perfect. But Isaac went on to have sons, one of which, Jacob, had twelve sons, one of which was Joseph. But, as we will see, the people still did not catch what God was trying to do, with them.

Fourth, God tried again when the people became slaves after the Period of the Patriarchs, which does not appear to be their fault. God sent them Moses, reinforced what He wanted with the Ten Commandments. He spared their children. Opened the Red Sea. He added support and warning of their leaders—God's Chosen. They failed again. These, too, fail, swamped in moral turpitude and civil war.

Fifth, while they had to fight and fight hard for it, He delivered them to the Promised Land, the Land of Canaan, flowing with milk and honey. Another Eden? Not quite. One thing led to another, and soon, tiringly predictable, they went their own way, "doing what was right in their own eyes. God had had enough, again. He disposes of them in bloody land battles in which Assyria, Babylonian and other countries attack God's chosen subjects, the "family" of Abraham. The Nation of Israel and its citizens are carted off to Babylonia—Exile.

Sixth, God saved them again. A handful of Jews are saved, called "The Remnant," large or small, as in the Flood-Noah-Ark scenario. They came back to Jerusalem. Great day in the morning! With passing years these survivors yield many more thousands. Another big, big population. However, these also flounder in spite of the Exodus, the Laws, the pleas and warnings of the prophets. God throws up His hands in dismay. "What shall I do next?"

It took a while to see. God's time is not our time, "Neither are your ways my ways," says the Lord. A thousand years, the Psalmist adds, are but as a watch in the night. Is that what Einstein knew? Time: relative, unending, moving, but back and forth, and not on man made timepiece, no a.m. or p.m., just God's time.

Seventh, God played His last card. His final decision was to come to earth Himself and rub shoulders with His people in the Presence of Jesus of Nazareth. God Himself came down. This is the "Blessing" factor, in fullness. Eventually it succeeds.

But it took a once-in-a-lifetime event to get the point across. The climax is represented in the contiguous acts of crucifixion, resurrection-ascension and the reappearances of Jesus after his temporal death. The Christian concept was born.

God spent the entire Old Testament, two thousand years of it, to reach His climax decision. He was very patient, and very determined, to succeed and attain his objective:

God in His infinite wisdom.
God in His infinite patience.

The Bible began in purity and peace—in the Garden of Eden. It also ends in purity and peace—in Heaven, where there are no tears, no sorrow, no sin, no separation—just like God, who like us, adores a happy ending.

The Lord's Mission and Challenge

God reached for His stylus and began to write.
God's job description:

To make mankind in my own image.
But not as a photographic replica.
"Image" in such sense as:

> With characteristics of.
> Kindred to.
> Representative of.
> To be an extension on earth of my philosophies and
policies.

Succinctly, and once again, the solution to this challenge is what the Bible texts are all about.

God in His infinite wisdom?
God in His infinite patience?

You think God could make a person as beautiful as you?
Of course, but not overnight.

Love, not shove.

God gave His proofs with the Resurrection and the reappearances.

The cost has been high in terms of human life...
The cost will remain high.

But the rewards are infinite and inviolate.

Adam and Eve.
Ark and Flood.
Promises and Blessings upon Abraham.
Ten Commandments.
Assyrian and Babylonian Devastations.
Presence of Jesus Christ.
Heaven, forever more.

FORECASTS BY PROPHETS
ABOUT JESUS

ISAIAH

Virgin Birth
"The virgin will be with child and will give birth to a son and will call him Immanuel, God with us.

MICAH 5:2

Bethlehem
"Out of you, Bethlehem, will come the one who will rule over Israel."

ISAIAH 9:1

Galilee
"He will honor (live in) Galilee."

ZECHARIAH

Branch
"I will bring forth my servant, the BRANCH."
(Translate "Branch" as Jesus Christ.)

JEREMIAH

David and A Righteous Branch
"The day is coming," declares the Lord, "when I will raise unto David a righteous Branch and a king who shall reign and prosper."
(Read "unto David" as, Up from the ancestry of King David.")
(Read "righteous Branch" as Jesus)

Spiritual Communion

Isaiah's passage,
Composed hand-in-hand with God,
Is a document
Sealed by witness,
Confirming a manifestation
Of the Communion of
The Holy Spirit with a human spirit.

This page closes Book One.

Jesus is being called to center stage.
Up front
Where He should be.

Jesus is simple.
And love.
So is God.
But sometimes He
Is a little harder to see.
Perhaps on purpose.

God says Jesus has been here forever.
"Same as me." (John 1:1)

Adult Jesus
Earth-time life,
Man-time ministry
Only three years.

But Jews had God,
or vice-versa,
Two thousand years
Before Jesus came.

Question:
Did God ever promise the Jews
Everlasting life
Before He came in the form of
Jesus Christ?

Would it have made
a difference?

* * * *

And so it came to pass.
Jesus Christ, our Lord, came to His people
and laid His foundations among them,
fixing His position at the pedestal of the Laws.
Several years later He moved
boldly and resolutely to his sacrifice
upon the cross,
offering His life as testimony
to His faith in the innate goodness of mankind.

Interlude
Window on Cloud 9

"Thank you for getting here so promptly," said the Lord, welcoming the two angels he had summoned.

The angels and the Lord were meeting in his spacious office high atop the Supreme Headquarters building at Universe Plaza. Zip Code: Cloud 9.

The Lord smiled graciously, noting the wondering excitement of the angels as their glances took in the lovely appointments. It was always a renewed thrill for them to come into His Presence.

"I see you are curious about that new item hanging on the wall," the Lord observed, following the angels' eyes. "Let me address your attention to it. It is a new calendar. I designed it myself.

"This new calendar shows today's date. As you see, it reads 5 B.C. I will explain it to you more fully later, and then you will understand about the 5 B.C. It refers to a new idea I have.

"Now let us address ourselves to today's order of business." The angels drew closer and waited for their Lord.

"A problem has come up to us. And as you will see, I must get a handle on it promptly. Let me explain.

"The problem originates," he continued, "with those Ten Laws we sent down many, many years ago. I am sure you remember the Ten Commandments. We sent them down to Moses when he was at Mount Sinai. My goodness, that was fourteen or fifteen hundred years ago.

"Well, it seems that our people have been having trouble living up to them. From time to time they break them and this of course gets them upset. And I think I can see why this is happening." The angels were listening closely to the Lord's words, attentive to the thrust of his presentation.

"No one is perfect," the Lord observed. "No one can do everything perfectly 100% of the time. But these Laws, the Ten Commandments, specify perfection, and, as such, they have been spread on the record and published.

"The result is a situation I had not at all intended. We have a conflict syndrome on our hands. You might think of it this way. An irresistible force has met a very-hard-to-move object. The result has been confusion, frustration and unhappiness among many of our people.

"It now looks like I had been over-confident. It appears I made a miscalculation. Come to think of it people, after all, are only human. Do you agree?" The angels looked at each other and smiled knowingly.

The Lord paused, reflecting.

"Now I have to reach a decision," he declared. "And I think I know what it is. First, though, I will tell you there is one action I cannot take. Besides this I have a second option. It is a fantastic idea that just may work.

"Give me a few days and I will summon you to me again." The angels departed, quietly and hopefully.

* * * *

Several days later the angels returned and the Lord announced, "I have made my decision. You remember the other day when I observed that our people were having difficulty with the Laws.

"Yes, it is true. The Laws are strict. Perhaps too confining for every reasonable every-day person to live with comfortably. In fact, the Laws may have actually become a burden in many cases.

"However, I have decided that I cannot strike down the Laws and withdraw them. The result would be chaos on earth. Besides, it would forever cloud my credibility. Any gains we have made would be forever lost. Such must not happen. Therefore, number one, the Laws remain in place."

One angel raised his hand, but the Lord waved him aside and hurried on. "Hear me out," he demanded. "This is what I am going to do. I am going to visit among our people myself. In human form, naturally. So that men and women can identify with me. See me. Hear me. Touch me. I will be called Jesus Christ. And when the time comes, each of you angels in turn will bestow these names upon me.

"In the name of Jesus Christ I will offer our people hope. I will promise my eternal love to them. Regardless of any transgressions they may have made. I will extend my hand and heart in forgiveness. I will reach them with a down-to-earth humanity.

"I will become a safety valve. I will be their safety net. Should anyone feel that he or she has failed, and thereupon comes to me, I will catch him in my arms and care for him or her.

"I will ask for nothing in return from them, except that they have absolute and unreserved faith and trust in me." The angels wept in their happiness.

And so it came to pass.
Jesus Christ, our Lord, came to his people
and laid his foundations among them,
fixing his position at the pedestal
of the Laws.
Several years later he moved
boldly and resolutely to his sacrifice
upon the cross,
offering his life as testimony
to his faith in the innate goodness of mankind.
Then, he went to be seated
at the right hand of God.

Book Two
THE NEW TESTAMENT

INTRODUCTION

Do not be alarmed. The New Testament, to Christians, is far more important than the Old, I guess. But there is far more to it, to be sure. Jesus Christ is the be-all and end-all.

Chapter I
THE PROLOGUE

The New Testament is a "pushover" by comparison to the Old. The Old Testament has three dozen heroes and a couple of girls. But the New has one Force, Jesus Christ, reflecting God's interests interacting shoulder to shoulder with man. Just one central character, Jesus, with all the events and dialogues between Him and His people, men and women.

Just one central theme: love, compassion, forgiveness. And, a promise, better than that if you will, a contract, offering everlasting-eternal life to follow physical, temporal, timely death of the body. Jesus adds, but it is not an ironbound condition, that if you support His demonstrated faith with your unreserved faith, His torture and sacrifice on the Cross will not have been an empty experience for Him, or for you. "Believe in Me," he said, and you will be with me in paradise!"

THE NEWER TESTAMENT

We are reaching our goal. The Blessing comes full circle. Jesus Christ is here. This part is His.

* * * *

Some of the copy below is impressionistic, some is blank verse, some is narrative prose. Some reads like a Sunday School lesson. The most effective compositions are no doubt my quotations directly from the Bible. If you ever have doubts about whether the Bible is helpful or true, I offer a simple solution. Read it!

Jesus is an elusive Being. Each of us must find Him in his or her own way. He will come to you as you find your path to Him. Jesus is so simple He can easily slip through your fingers unless you are especially careful. Jesus is Love, start to finish.

Many robed, silver-haired theologians have tried to explain and identify Jesus in modern-time terms. They fail. Their examinations wind up as on a carousel. Jesus is a mystery, until you in your way, catch and hold Him, or rather until He catches and holds you!

"Ask, and it will be given you. Seek, and you shall find." This is Jesus. Ask Him in your most private, heart-tearing prayer. He will come to you. This is Jesus.

GOD COMES DOWN TO EARTH.

If this is the first time you have come
face to face
with this reality,
it should make you gasp.

In black and white
blue sky, brown earth
JESUS CHRIST WAS GOD WALKING ON EARTH.

If you are startled,
join the crowd.

It is a stunning idea.
It is an astonishing proposition.

It is more than these.

It actually happened.

THE SECRET OF JESUS

The phenomenon of God's being on earth in human form is a mystery.

For two thousand years wondering minds have said, "It just could not happen." They reach this conclusion because they know no human-experience explanation for it.

Yet the basic evidence that it did happen is recorded in the Bible. Confirmed by many witnesses. Matthew, Mark, Luke, John, Paul, Peter, and James, as separate individuals, each entered his own record under diverse circumstances and years apart. Each confirms the other, although widely differing in their details.

Their stories are close enough and yet vary enough to reinforce the sincerity and validity of their individual observations. If their records were too close a match, they would be suspect.

If you cannot explain the Jesus-event in terms of human experience, why not try a supernatural hypothesis? It may help unravel the problem.

THE POWER OF JESUS

First, you are confronted with a vast power unlike anything known on earth. There is recorded factual evidence of this power. The miracles performed by Jesus Christ. Thirty-five or more. They are cited and recorded by Matthew, Mark, Luke and John. Lazarus brought back to life from four days dead, by a command of Christ. An epileptic boy cured with the touch of a hand. Such incidents are not optical illusions nor tricks of the mind. They are factual reality, dealing with human cells and flesh.

The Power is invisible, intangible, intuitive and apparently limitless. It is also transferable. Bestowable.

You may ground the creation of Jesus in the divine Power factor. The Power, which we call "God," touched to life the egg-ovum in the mother's body. The baby developed, the child became Jesus and then became the man, Jesus Christ.

Sometimes Jesus called Himself a Son of Man. In a sense He was. A son of Mankind. He also called Himself the Son of God. He was that, too.

MIRROR - IMAGE

Somewhere during Jesus' development the Supreme Power—God—transfused His omnipotence into the Being of Jesus. The Almighty duplicated His Force in his son. John says in his Gospel that they both were there at the moment of creation. Later, much later, Christ came down.

The power within Jesus became the mirror-image of the supreme power we call God. God created life. Jesus returned dead persons to the living.

This circumstance gives us two manifestations of the divine power:

ONE: God the Father
TWO: Jesus Christ, the Son

The Third Dimension

The Holy Spirit is the third dimension of the divine power concept. He performs as the conduit of the Power. He is an invisible energy transmission line. When God releases His power toward a situation, the Holy Spirit is the channel that carries the energy flow. A divine beam of energy, representing, as he promised, Jesus the Christ, and...representing God!

THREE   Father, Son, Holy Spirit.
TRINITY
     These three are the components of the power-ene structure...
There are three who command the helm in heaven.
They are:
The Father
Jesus Christ, the Son
The Holy Ghost (or Spirit - to be modern)

"These three are One."
{John 5:7)

THE GENTLE TOUCH OF THE POWER

Should you ever feel suffused with a release of
God's power within you—many people report this
experience—if only for a passing moment,
The Holy Spirit is the instrument
which has carried the Power unto you.

Sometimes such incident is called an "Illumination."
It is unique and unforgettable.
It is transporting.
It releases all tensions.
It bestows healing peace.

You have been blessed.
Some people call it being
Born Again, others call it
A new beginning. It does not
Matter what you call it—
It is here—for you.

As it was for me
Several times, some
Recently, I have been
Visited by God. I
Have seen the Lord!

Chapter II
A PROFILE

"Who can I turn to,
should you turn away? . . ."

After the Old Book, the New Testament verses are a joyful, rollicking roller-coaster ride. Reams of lyrical writing, page after page, mirror God's high spirits. Much of it, if not all, is His handiwork. The Lord is swinging-free at His inspiring, animated best.

Quoted below is an even-tempered passage, describing various events and actions of Jesus Christ's daily routine during the early portion of His ministry. The verses introduce the circumstances leading to Jesus' delivery of the celebrated Sermon on the Mount.

A Typical Day in the Life of Jesus Christ

"Jesus went through Galilee, teaching in synagogues, preaching the good news of the Kingdom, and healing disease and sickness among the people. News about him spread all over Syria, and people brought to him all who were ill with various diseases, those suffering severe pain, the demon-possessed, the epileptics and the paralytics, and he healed them. Large crowds from Galilee, the Decapolis (The Ten Cities), Jerusalem, Judea and the region across the Jordan followed him."

MATTHEW 4:23-25

BOOKS OF THE NEW TESTAMENT

Gospels | Matthew
Mark
Luke
John (Zebedee)

* * * *

Apostles | The Acts

* * * *

Paul's Letters | Romans
I Corinthians
II Corinthians

Galatians
Ephesians
Philippians
Colossians

I Thessalonians
II Thessalonians
I Timothy
II Timothy
Titus
Philemon

* * * *

Hebrews (author unknown)

James (Jesus' brother)
I Peter
II Peter
I John (above)
II John
III John
Jude

Revelation (John)

The principal objective of the New Testament volume is the story of Jesus Christ...

The first four books tell of Jesus' life. These works are the "Gospels," meaning Good News. The book of Acts (Acts of the Apostles) was also written by Luke. Acts picks up following Christ's resurrection and traces how the power of the Holy Spirit supports the evangelical missions of Peter and John, the Apostle Paul, with Mark and others at hand. Matthew, Mark and Luke are chronologies of events. John amplifies the spiritual aspects of Jesus. Mark is considered the earliest book of the Gospels, then Matthew, Luke and later John.

* * * *

The next thirteen books of the New Testament are letters by Paul written to people in countries and cities outside the holy lands, such as Greece and Italy. They are sales presentations, promoting and justifying the meaning and desirability of Jesus Christ's philosophy of living...which boils down to the word "LOVE." The final books: two by Peter (the famous disciple-apostle), one each by Jude and James, the brother of Jesus, one by a Jerusalem rabbi, and four by John (above) closing with John's "Revelation," which is a bible in itself. The author of Hebrews is unknown.

I know there is large disagreement among scholars about who wrote what, but I find it easier to stay with the traditional authors.

The Gospelliers!

As I ventured through my journey, I have become friendly with these four fellows of old; Matthew, Mark, Luke and John, and I think they have become friendly with me. At least they were willing to share their individual secrets (or purposes) in why they wrote the Gospels they wrote: four stories about one man.

Anyone who reads them can tell that they differ, especially if you read them closely. Each had a special purpose. I should not pretend to be a Grecian Scholar (they wrote their stories in Greek), but I discovered, with a little help from my friends, the following:

(1) Matthew is a Jew, or was. I mean to say by that he was writing primarily for his own people: the Jews. He was trying to persuade them that Jesus was the Christ, their long awaited Messiah. He keeps telling them how the Old Testament prophecies we mentioned are fulfilled in the New. He had to tell his story, but he was saying, in shorthand: The wait is over. He is here. Jesus is the Messianic Christ! Amen.

(2) Mark, the first Gospel written is the shortest and in my opinion, the easiest to understand. Simple, direct and to the point. Mark did not like to embellish things. He tells us what he knew. No angelic birth announcements; no wisemen or shepherds at the manger; no visitations by the risen Christ...Just a good God-man Jesus who came to tell us how to live, to die to forgive us of our sins, and to show us how to live forever more. I especially like Mark, my kind of man.

(3) Luke, who also wrote the Acts, is a gentile (non-Jew) writing to the gentile world, especially, as he mentions, to one Theophilus. His is a non-Jewish gospel. Someone told me he was writing to show the Roman, Greek speaking world, that Jesus and his followers were simple, God-loving people, who helped the poor, led good lives, and took care of others and themselves. There was no need to fear them for they were men and women of peace, not war. The Emperor need not fear them. Luke majors in parables and miracles. I like him, too.

(4) John is everybody's favorite of the four, but I find him complicated and too much concerned with the last week of Jesus' life. Could be he is right, but I prefer the gentler stories of Luke, the simple hard hitting reports of Mark and even the Sermon on The Mount in Matthew. Not that John is without merit. Check your remembered knowledge of what you know of Jesus. Much of it, I guess, comes from John. He is the prince of the gospel writers.

THE ACTS OF THE APOSTLES

Luke's volume two begins with the Ascension of Jesus into Heaven—much more detailed than anywhere else. It then goes on to a peaceful group of Christians who gave up everything they owned to share it with the others. Then it covers Peter and his great Pentecostal Sermon. Then soon Paul moves in to dominate the book. From Saul-Paul's Conversion in chapter nine, Peter and John disappear. It is a gentile book.

PAUL'S LETTERS

No one knows for sure how many of the thirteen letters attributed to Paul, Paul actually wrote. Some he surely did. Others he most likely did not. It really doesn't matter all that much to you and me.

All are sure he wrote *Romans,* a massive theological statement of the New Testament Christian faith, possibly the best theological book ever written, concise by standards of the theological books I know of. Everything is there. If you have time for only one Pauline letter, read Romans.

If you like spice and moral problems, even a young man making love to his father's second wife (it's there!), or good Christians coming early to communion and drinking all the wine before the service even began (that's there too), then read *I and II Corinthians,* especially the first one where most of the sins of man and woman are unveiled and directions given for a good and holy life. As I asked, as did the preacher author of Ecclesiastes: "Is anything new under the sun?"

I like to read Paul's letters. They are alive and to the point. The points were often different then, but I usually find myself and my shortcomings hoisted on a New Testament Petard.

The letters to the Thessalonians are to the point of what happens when we die. The letters to Timothy tell us what

St. Paul had to say to an up and coming young leader of the Church.

Each of the others has a special point or two; please read them. Think of it as a wise friend, relaying what he has found important about the Christ and the Christian life.

* * * *

THE LETTERS OF JOHN AND PETER

One wise old scholar told me bluntly that John and Peter did not write their letters. Well, I suppose he was right, in the sense that he was historically accurate, but pardon my naivete when I tell you I find them easier to read and listen to when I assume that John and Peter wrote them. Perhaps you should do the same.

* * * *

Now there are other miscellaneous New Testament books which you should read: Hebrews is a lovely book about high priests and the cloud of witnesses in the heavens who cheer us on. James, written I think by the brother of our Lord, emphasizes correct and proper behavior for the Christian. Titus, Jude and Philemon are slightly enigmatic to me, especially as to why they were included in the Canon; but at least they are short and easy to read.

THE REVELATION TO JOHN

The last book of the Bible, largely a mystery to me with its wild visions and incomprehensible creatures, is technically an apocalypse. That means it is a disclosure of the future, a revelation of things to come. Christ sends selective messages to seven churches. They all had problems, such as we.

The detail is fascinating to say the least. The main message is that Christ will one day win the world for Himself. A new heaven and a new earth will come.

Revelations sparks my imaginations. Like chapter 21:10-21:

And in the Spirit he carried me away to a great, high mountain, and showed me the holy city Jerusalem coming down out of heaven from God, having the glory of God, its radiance like a most rare jewel, like a jasper, clear as crystal. It had a great, high wall, with twelve gates, and at the gates twelve angels, and on the gates the names of the twelve tribes of the sons of Israel were inscribed; on the east three gates, on the north three gates, on the south three gates, and on the west three gates. And the wall of the city had twelve foundations, and on them the twelve names of the twelve apostles of the Lamb.

And he who talked to me had a measuring rod of gold to measure the city and its gates and walls. The city lies foursquare, its length the same as its breadth; and he measured the city with his rod, twelve thousand stadia; its length and breadth and height are equal. He also measured its wall, a hundred and forty-four cubits by a man's measure, that is, an angel's. The wall was built of jasper, while the city was pure gold, clear as glass. The foundations of the wall of the city were adorned with every jewel; the first was jasper, the second sapphire, the third agate, the fourth emerald, the fifth onyx, the sixth carnelian, the seventh chrysolite, the eighth beryl, the ninth topaz, the tenth chrysoprase, the eleventh jacinth, the twelfth amethyst. And the twelve gates were twelve pearls, each of the gates made of a single pearl, and the street of the city was pure gold, transparent as glass.

And 22:1-5:

> Then he showed me the river of the water of life, bright as crystal, flowing from the throne of God and of the Lamb through the middle of the street of the city; also, on either side of the river, the tree of life with its twelve kinds of fruit, yielding its fruit each month; and the leaves of the tree were for the healing of the nations. There shall no more be anything accursed, but the throne of God and of the Lamb shall be in it, and his servants shall worship him: they shall see his face, and his name shall be on their foreheads. And night shall be no more; they need no light of lamp or sun, for the Lord God will be their light, and they shall reign for ever and ever.

And 21:1-4 brings lovely succor to the tired men and women growing older:

> Then I saw a new heaven and a new earth; for the first heaven and the first earth had passed away, and the sea was no more. And I saw the holy city, new Jerusalem, coming down out of heaven from God, prepared as a bride adorned for her husband; and I heard a loud voice from the throne saying, "Behold, the dwelling of God is with men. He will dwell with them, and they shall be his people, and God himself will be with them; he will wipe away every tear from their eyes, and death shall be no more, neither shall there be mourning nor crying nor pain any more, for the former things have passed away."

22:18-19 carries the severest warning:

> I warn every one who hears the words of the prophecy of this book: if any one adds to them, God will add to him the plagues described in this book, and if any one takes away from the words of the book of this prophecy, God will take away his share in the tree of life and in the holy city, which are described in this book.

And, the last word is the finest and the best, Rev 22:20-21:

> He who testifies to these things says, "Surely I am coming soon." Amen. Come, Lord Jesus! The grace of the Lord Jesus be with all the saints. Amen.

JESUS WAS GOD

Very few persons
come to grips
with the actuality that
Jesus Christ was God.
And those who do
are often so self-righteous

It is an assertion that
thunders with challenge.

It says, "I dare you..."

* * * *

Now you would like to see proofs.

Accordingly, this essay has contacted
two top correspondents
to address the matter.

They are Saint John and Saint Paul,
distinguished veterans of Jesus Christ's campaign.

They knew Jesus well.

John reports, live action, Jesus' verbal exchanges
when confronting a crowd. Paul reports in the
form of a letter.

John Reports:
   Jesus is being challenged
   by a crowd in Jerusalem.
  "IF THOU BE THE CHRIST, TELL US STRAIGHT OUT."

   Jesus comes back with a one-liner...
   'I AND MY FATHER ARE ONE."

John Reports:
   The crowd is aroused. People cry out.
   "MORE. WE WANT MORE EVIDENCE."

   Jesus hammers back at them:
  "THE MIRACLES I HAVE DONE BEAR WITNESS.
   THEY ARE MY EVIDENCE.
   I CARRY MY FATHER'S POWER."

John Reports:
   The crowd becomes belligerent. It surges.
   "YOU ARE A LIAR. PROVE YOU ARE GOD'S SON."

   Jesus' face becomes hard. He thrusts back:
   "BELIEVE YOUR OWN EYES.
  MY MIRACLES STARE YOU IN THE FACE.
  SEE THEM AND YOU SEE MY POWER.
   MY FATHER'S POWER IS IN ME.
   MY FATHER AND I ARE ONE."

   Sources:
   JOHN 10:24, 25, 30, 33, 38

John Reports:
   Scene: The Last Supper. Jesus is exchanging
  final questions and answers with the disciples
   on the eve of His crucifixion.

Jesus speaks:
"Do not be troubled.
In my Father's realm
Are many mansions.
We have a place for you there."

Disciple THOMAS asks:
"LORD, HOW WILL WE KNOW THE WAY?"

Jesus explains:
"No man comes to my Father's realm alone.
I will lead you there...
If YOU KNOW ME, YOU KNOW MY FATHER.
YOU HAVE SEEN ME.
THEREFORE, YOU HAVE SEEN HIM.
I AM THE WAY."

Source:
JOHN 14:2-7

Another disciple asks:
"LORD, SHOW US THE FATHER."

Jesus answers:
"PHILIP. Take another look.
I have been with you a long time.
HE WHO HAS SEEN ME HAS SEEN THE FATHER.

I do not tell you these things on my own say-so.
IT IS MY FATHER LIVING IN ME
WHO SAYS THESE WORDS.
I AM AS ONE WITH MY FATHER.
MY FATHER AND I ARE AS ONE."

Source:
JOHN 14:8-11

Do the dramatized sequences unsettle you?
This experience is no sentimental dream.
It is real-life. Hard as nails.

Jesus' lines have been in the Book
Two thousand years.

Waiting for you.

Now they are yours.

* * * *

Paul reports:
If you prefer a quieter tone, Paul's exhibit
Says it succinctly
And with precision.

In a letter to the citizens of Philippi, Greece
Paul explains to his readers what is meant by

The Presence of Jesus Christ

A BEING...
...Who in pure form was God.
...Who had God's powers within him.
...Who was blessed to exercise God's powers.
...Who was made in the form of human likeness.
...Who was in appearance a man.

Source:
PHILIPPIANS 2:5-8

THE BEAUTITUDES

"Now when he saw the crowds, he went up on a mountainside and sat down. His disciples came to him, and he began to teach them saying:

"Blessed are the poor in spirit,
　　for theirs is the kingdom of heaven.
Blessed are those who mourn,
　　for they will be comforted.
Blessed are the meek,
　　for they will inherit the earth.
Blessed are those who hunger and
　　thirst for righteousness,
　　for they will be filled.
Blessed are the merciful,
　　for they will be shown mercy.
Blessed are the pure in heart,
　　for they will see God.
Blessed are the peacemakers,
　　for they will be called sons of God.
Blessed are those who are persecuted
　　because of righteousness,
　　for theirs is the kingdom of heaven."

MATTHEW 5:3-10

From the Sermon on the Mount

"You are the light of the world. A city set on a hill cannot be hid. Nor do men light a lamp and put it under a bushel, but on a stand, and it gives light to all in the house. Let your light so shine before men, that they may see your good works and give glory to your Father who is in heaven."

MATTHEW 5:14-16

The Ten Commandments
(New Testament Version)

"Do not think that I have come to abolish the Law or the Prophets; I have not come to abolish them."

"Anyone who breaks one of the least of these commandments and teaches others to do the same will be called least in the kingdom of heaven, but whoever practices and teaches these commands will be called great in the kingdom of heaven."

MATTHEW 5:17, 19

How You Should Pray

"When you pray, go into your room, close the door and pray to your Father, who is unseen. Then your Father, who sees what is done in secret, will reward you. And when you pray, do not keep on babbling like pagans, for they think they will be heard because of their many words. Do not be like them, for your Father knows what you need before you ask him.

"This is how you should pray:

"Our Father in heaven,
hallowed be Your name,
Your kingdom come,
Your will be done
　　on earth as it is in heaven.
Give us today our daily bread.
Forgive us our debts,
　　as we also have forgiven our debtors.
And lead us not into temptation,
　　but deliver us from the evil."

MATTHEW 6:7-13

Criticizing Others

"Judge not, that you be not judged. For with the judgement you pronounce you will be judged, and the measure you give will be the measure you get. Why do you see the speck that is in your brother's eye, but do not notice the log that is in your own eye? You hypocrite, first take the log out of your own eye, and then you will see clearly to take the speck out of your brother's eye."

Matthew 7:1-5

Seek and Receive

"Ask and it will be given to you; seek and you will find; knock and the door will be opened to you. For everyone who asks receives; he who seeks finds; and to him who knocks, the door will be opened.

"Which of you, if his son asks for bread will give him a stone? Or if he asks for a fish, will give him a snake?

When you know how to give good gifts to your children, how much more will your Father in heaven give good gifts to those who ask him! In everything, do to others what you would have them do to you, for this sums up the Law and the Prophets."

Matthew 7:7-12

The Sensible Builder

"Therefore everyone who hears these words of mine and puts them into practice is like a wise man who built his house on the rock. The rain came down, the streams rose, and the winds blew and beat against that house; yet it did not fall, because it had its foundation on the rock. But everyone who hears these words of mine and does not put them into practice is like a foolish man who built his house on sand. The rain came down, the streams rose, and the winds blew and beat against that house, and it fell with a great crash."

Matthew 7:24-27

One more selection, below, exhibits more passages familiar to you. Its force bears the mark of the inspiration of the Lord. Composed two thousand years ago, this remarkable script stands unique and distinguished in concept, content and composition among all efforts of creative published literature. "Love" is as fresh and nourishing today as it was twenty centuries ago.

LOVE. Expressed by Saint Paul. Circa 50 A.D.
I Corinthians 13 (RSV)

If I speak in the tongues of men and of angels, but have not love, I am a noisy gong or a clanging cymbal. And if I have prophetic powers, and understand all mysteries and all knowledge, and if I have all faith, so as to remove mountains, but have not love, I am nothing. If I give away all I have, and if I deliver my body to be burned, but have not love, I gain nothing.

Love is patient and kind; love is not jealous or boastful; it is not arrogant or rude. Love does not insist on its own way; it is not irritable or resentful; it does not rejoice at wrong, but rejoices in the right. Love bears all things, believes all things, hopes all things, endures all things.

Love never ends; as for prophecies, they will pass away; as for tongues, they will cease; as for knowledge, it will pass away. For our knowledge is imperfect and our prophecy is imperfect; but when the perfect comes, the imperfect will pass away. When I was a child, I spoke like a child, I thought like a child, I reasoned like a child; when I became a man, I gave up childish ways. For now we see in a mirror dimly, but then face to face. Now I know in part; then I shall understand fully, even as I have been fully understood. So faith, hope, love abide, these three; but the greatest of these is love.

Celebration

Jesus Christ was born in the Spring.
When a new sun
Was warming the earth.

No, that may not be quite correct.

Jesus Christ was born at Christmas Time.
Christmas Day.

No, that is not quite right either.

* * * *

Jesus came by the Grace of God
Before there was a Christmas Day.

His Celebration day was chosen long later.
Much longer later.

* * * *

There was no New Testament then,
When Jesus Christ came.
There was no prompting script
Ready to guide Him.

Jesus constructed the text.
And it became His Celebration.

Today, it is our Celebration.
And, forever more, too.

When Jesus Christ came,
Earth was quiet.
God had not spoken for four hundred years.

At Mary and Joseph's primitive manger-crib
His Bethlehem birth was hailed by
Three traveling kings from distant lands...
The Magi.

An angel whispered to little Mary
Then sang to the shepherds in their fields
The Inn-Keeper said, "We're full."
Herod chased the baby with
His parents, off to Egypt.
The three came back. Then....

* * * *

The people of Jesus Christ's day
Were the same people of Moses' day;
Or of King David's day
One thousand years later.

Perhaps somewhat more chastened
Following the ordeal
Of hundreds of years
Of painful tests and terrible punishments.

* * * *

In Jesus time
These people numbered
About three million.

Their landscape was arid,
Their minds were dry.
Their spirits thirsted.

* * * *

To a people bearing centuries of
Ingrained conditioning
He was indeed a stranger.

Jesus was new. Unique.

* * * *

God had come Himself
To mediate and arbitrate.
To speak for Himself
To act on Man's behalf...
But few "crossed the line"
To commit and sign
God's new contract,
Tendered by Jesus.

He came offering water.
Many tasted His cup.

And came away...wondering.

Despite numerous personal, tender and moving encounters
Between Jesus and souls of everyday grade,
Recorded again and again
In Matthew, Mark, Luke and John,
These were not enough
To ignite a Christian crusade,
Not that we know of.

The Gospels cite instances of a
Ground-swell response by the masses.
As many as 5,000 beings, addressed and fed
By Jesus with "five loaves, two fish."
But the momentum gained
Did not mature and roll.

* * * *

In several instances the flames flared.
Many times hot coals seared and healed.

Jesus' fire burned its brightest
When they tried to put it out.

But His was an eternal fire
To ignite anew
At another place, another time.

SUMMATION

Jesus is simple.
And love.

So is God.
But sometimes He
Is a little harder to see.
Perhaps on purpose.

God says Jesus has been here forever.
"Same as me." (JOHN 1:1)

Adult Jesus
Earth-time life,
Man-time ministry
Only three years.

But Jews had God,
or vice-versa,
Two thousand years
Before Jesus came.

Question:
Did God ever promise the Jews
Everlasting life
Before He came in the form of
Jesus Christ?

Would it have made
a difference?

I think He did, after all
An everlasting Blessing is a
long, long time.

A Statement about a Problem
"I Dare You!"

Most people at a church service accept the phenomenon of Jesus Christ compliantly and obediently. They receive Him with reverence and respect. His comforting words reassure, encourage and inspire.

The question is how many persons in a Sunday congregation come to grips with the actuality that Jesus Christ was God walking on earth in human form? This is a proposition that thunders with challenge. It says, "I dare you..."

* * * *

The minister speaks from his pulpit and the people listen.

But do they hear?

What do they hear?

Are they translating?

Translating? Probably they are not because their minds are not prepared with information. Their brains and experience have only an indistinct frame of reference, a shadowy background around which to orient.

They do not have an encompassing perspective of the Bible chronicle. Yes, they know many of its individual parts and special events. They are familiar with many passages. But at best they have only a tenuous intellectual grasp of the whole. They do not see the forest for the trees.

The clergyman speaks.
The people listen.
Is the drama of Jesus Christ's words real to them?
Do the realities come to bear?
Are they translating?
Two thousand years was a long, long time ago.
More likely they are hearing
a hum, a murmur
of a distant, nebulous, elusive sound.
Translation cannot be done with a naked imagination.
One must dress his mind with knowledge.
You must know the life-experience and heritage
of Jesus Christ to feel the force
and reap the impact of His message.

Confront the matter.

CONCLUSION

Well, reader friend, our journey is through. But God's journey with us is not. The blessing continues far into the night and far far into the future. What heavenly realms await us, where we can stroll along for a million years with Abraham, Moses, David, Isaiah, Paul, Peter and of course Jesus The Christ.

Time is gone. It is not of the essence over there. Standing at the gates is one who knows your name. He will not trot out a long list of the faults and failures. His memory is brief in that regard.

The Bible says he will remember how hard you tried, the successes you had, the lives you touched. The journey is such that when Christ comes to you (and to me) He takes us by the hand and leads us through the gates: forgiven and renewed.

It's true. Believe it! Enjoy it! For now and ever more. Amen

B1
W

Whitlock, James P.

4380

"My Adventures with
Mankind"

ST. JOHNS EPISCOPAL CHURCH
211 N. MONROE STREET
TALLAHASSEE, FL 32303

DESERT MINISTRIES, INC.
Box 2001
Fort Lauderdale, Florida 33303

or

Box 13235
Pittsburgh, Pennsylvania 15243